CW01306626

From Anxiety to Authenticity

The Creative Entrepreneurs' guide for Mental Health and Wellbeing mixing Therapy, Philosophy, and Practical Wisdom

Nikola Steinhope

Contents

Introduction: Outlining the Journey to Creative Entrepreneurial Thriving ... 1
    Overview of the Book's Mission for Creative Entrepreneurs ... 1
    The Importance of Mental Resilience in the Creative Industry. ... 2

Chapter 1: The Creative Mind: Understanding the Unique Mental Health Challenges Faced by the Entrepreneurial Artist ... 4
    Understanding Anxiety ... 4
    The Link Between Creativity and Anxiety ... 5
    How Anxiety Affects the Entrepreneurial Journey ... 6
    Identifying Personal Anxiety Triggers ... 6
    The Role of Past Experiences ... 7
    The Entrepreneurial Environment ... 8
    Therapeutic Insights on Creative Anxiety ... 9
    Self-Care for Creative Entrepreneurs ... 10
    Managing Self-Doubt and Imposter Syndrome ... 10
    Overcoming Creative Blocks ... 11

Chapter 2: Balancing Work and Personal Life as a Creative Entrepreneur ... 13
    Creative Work-Life Challenges ... 13
    Priority Setting & Boundaries ... 14
    Sustainable Well-being Routines ... 15
    Supportive Networks & Mentors ... 15
    Nurturing Connections & Relationships ... 16

Chapter 3: Balancing Passion and Practicality in the Creative Journey ... 18
    Exploring the Balance of Artistic Passion and Practicality ... 18
    Finding and Sustaining Inspiration ... 19
    Therapy in Decision-Making ... 19
    Reflections on Finding Harmony Between Passion and Practicality ... 20

Chapter 4: The Rollo May Approach: Building a Foundation for Self-Determination ... 22
    Rollo May: Existential Anxiety, Creativity & Artistic Entrepreneurship ... 22
    Empowering creative entrepreneurs to define their paths independently. ... 23
    Techniques to Break Free from Societal Expectations ... 23
    Practical Tips to Harnessing Struggle for Creative Expression ... 24

Chapter 5: Redefining Success: the Philosophical Shift ... 26
    Philosophical Insights on Redefining Success in the Creative Realm ... 26
    Encouraging a Shift from External Validation to Intrinsic Fulfillment ... 27
    Authentic Goal-Setting Strategies ... 28

Chapter 6: Overcoming Obstacles and Persevering in the Creative Field — 29
- Developing Resilience and Persistence — 29
- Embracing Adaptability in the Creative Industry — 30
- Celebrating Successes and Personal Growth — 31

Chapter 7: Handling Criticism and Rejection — 32
- Philosophical Exploration of Rejection and Failure — 32
- Coping Mechanisms for Handling Criticism and Rejection — 33
- Principles for Maintaining Confidence and Self-Worth — 34
- Transformative Perspectives on Constructive Feedback — 34

Chapter 8: Embracing Failure and Growth — 36
- Failure as a Natural Part of the Creative Process — 36
- Strategies for Reframing Failure as a Catalyst for Success — 37
- Failures and Strategic Shifts in Art History — 38

Chapter 9: Nurturing Creativity and Inspiration in Everyday Life — 39
- Embracing a growth mindset and continuous learning — 39
- Fostering Creativity through Environment and Workspace Design — 39
- The Art of Balancing Rest and Productivity for Creative Success — 41
- Exercises for a Growth Mindset — 42

Chapter 10: Authenticity in Creative Entrepreneurship — 44
- Understanding Authenticity — 44
- The Relationship between Authenticity and Anxiety — 45
- Authentic Leadership — 45
- Steps to Becoming More Authentic — 46
- Building an Authentic Brand — 47
- Authenticity and Business Success — 48

Chapter 11: Enhancing Productivity and Creativity — 51
- Time Management for Creative Entrepreneurs — 51
- Goal-Setting Strategies for Effective Work — 52
- Cultivating a Creative Mindset — 53
- Creative Brainstorming Exercises — 54
- Boosting Creativity and Productivity — 55

Chapter 12: Self-Care Practices for Creative Entrepreneurs — 57
- Self-Care Balancing Work and Wellbeing — 57
- Building Healthy Routines and Boundaries — 57
- Mindfulness and Self-Reflection — 58
- Beating Burnout: Sustainable Creativity — 59
- Therapeutic Stress Management — 60
- Philosophical Reflections on a Sustainable Creative Lifestyle — 61

Chapter 13: Breaking Free from Comparison Traps — 63
- Comparison Traps in Historical Perspective — 63
- Embracing Individuality in the Creative Journey — 65
- Therapeutic Perspectives on Managing Comparison Struggles — 65

Self-Acceptance and Uniqueness: Practical Exercises 66

Chapter 14: Therapy Toolbox for Creative Minds — 68
Tailored Therapies for Creative Entrepreneurship 68
Techniques for Stress Management 69
Exercises for Improving Self-Awareness and a Positive Mindset 70

Chapter 15: Resilience in Uncertain Times: Thriving Through Challenges — 72
Embracing Life's Challenges 72
Therapeutic Strategies for Uncertainty and Ambiguity 73
History, Creativity and Adversity 73

Chapter 16: Building Resilient Relationships in the Creative Community — 75
Fostering Collaborative Relationships 75
Addressing Challenges Through Communication 76
Networking Tips for Building a Creative Community 77

Chapter 17: Mindful Marketing: Authenticity in Promotion — 78
Authentic Marketing 78
Value-Aligned Promotional Strategies 79
Marketing and Promoting Creative Work Effectively 80

Chapter 18: Overcoming Financial Challenges and Building a Sustainable Creative Career — 82
Financial Fundamentals 82
Money Mangement and Planning 83
Focusing Anxiety to Practical Chores in Finance 84
Tax and Legal Matters 84
Building a Financial Safety Net - Saving and Investing for the Future 85
Diversifying Income and Revenue Sources 86
Thriving in a Creative Career 87
Practical Financial Planning for Creatives 88

Chapter 19: Cultivating a Positive Mindset and Wellbeing — 90
Overcoming Perfectionism 90
Cultivating gratitude and Joy in the Creative Process 91
Focus on Physical Health and Wellness 92
Seeking Professional Support 92

Chapter 20: Sustaining Thriving: Long-Term Strategies for Creative Entrepreneurs — 94
Building Longevity Self-Care Habits 94
Creating a Long-Term Motivation Plan 95
Cultivating a Creative Community 96
Self-Reflection and Growth 97

Final Chapter: Thriving Beyond Limits: a Call to Action — 98
The Potential for Creative Entrepreneurs to Thrive. 98
A Call to Action to for Mixing Therapy, Philosophy, and Practical wisdom 99

Share this Newfound Knowledge with the Creative Community 99

Introduction: Outlining the Journey to Creative Entrepreneurial Thriving

Overview of the Book's Mission for Creative Entrepreneurs

To all who've dared to weave their creative dreams, artistic passions and talent gifts into the fabric of their lives, this book is for you. Every artist who has taken the leap of faith to marry their creativity with entrepreneurship—the ones who passionately sketch their masterpieces in the silence of the night after an exhausting day bustling at work, this is a guide to help you on your journey. This book's purpose, is to guide you, trailing into a career in creative entrepreneurship in it's varied instantiations, to stride from merely coping to truly thriving. The world's stage is not kind to the script of the artist, and often the struggle takes its toll as you juggle the demands of the market with your deep-seated need for creative expression. Herein lies this book's raison d'être—to usher you from the shadows of anxiety to the brilliance of authenticity, a state of mind where your creativity and entrepreneurial spirit can coexist harmoniously.

But what does thriving truly look like for a creative entrepreneur? It's more than just surviving the storm; it's learning to dance in the rain. It's embracing your unique blend of creativity and business acumen as a master craft. Thriving means harnessing the twirling tempest of your anxiety, embracing it, moulding it, and allowing it to fuel your journey. It's understanding that your best work blossoms from your truest self, unfettered by the spectres of self-doubt. Thriving is not a destination to be achieved but rather an ongoing process, a tension between our inner world and the external one. It's a dynamic state where our mental resilience is as significant as our creative brilliance. It's about finding solace in therapy, wisdom in philosophy, and strategic insights from entrepreneurial experience. Learning, unlearning, and relearning in order to shape our authenticity and weave a story from a maelstrom of challenges and triumphs.

Through the pages of this book, we'll delve into the labyrinth of your unique mental landscape, traversing the valleys of anxiety, ascending the peaks of creativity, and finding a serene plateau where the two can reconcile. We'll wrestle with existential questions, dissect therapeutic concepts, probe philosophical wisdom, and unpack strategic insights from creative entrepreneurs of history.

Do not shy away from the dark corners of your psyche, for within those concealed crevices lie the keys to your creative liberation.

While the path of the creative entrepreneur can often feel lonely, ensnared by insecurities that whisper in the quiet moments, this journey is only as solitary as you allow it to be. The shared human experience, an act of solidarity in the face of adversity, and an affirmation of our collective resilience.

Take a moment to marvel at your courage. You've dared to dialogue with your dreams, leaned into your passion and challenged the conventional to carve a niche for your creative spirit. Yours is a path less traversed, a voyage as inspiring as it is intimidating. Remember, every stroke of the brush, every note in melody, every word in verse—each can be a declaration of defiance against homogeneity, an assertion of authenticity and innovation. As you embark on this journey from anxiety to authenticity, remember that you are not alone. You are proceeded by fellow travellers. As you turn the pages, you'll find pieces of wisdom etched with empathy, courage bound with contemplation and strategic insights.

Let this discourse not only illuminate your path but also serve as a gentle reminder that your uniqueness, your authentic self is the lifeblood of your journey, the muse for your creative spirit and the cornerstone of your entrepreneurial endeavour. Tread with courage, for no one else can walk the path that lies before you. Only you can meld the whispering winds of your creativity with the roaring currents of entrepreneurship, forming a symphony that resonates with both your heart and commercial success. This is your odyssey. Welcome to your journey from merely coping to genuinely thriving.

The Importance of Mental Resilience in the Creative Industry.

At first glance, mental resilience might strike you as a bit of an outlier in the creative industry where celebrated traits often rest on the triad of originality, passion, and skill. However, under its quiet surface powers a truly formidable engine that fuels creativity amidst adversity and anchors stability in the face of change. This foundational strength is the life essence of every pioneering artist, every innovative entrepreneur. It sets apart thriving creative minds from those consumed by their own sparks of genius.

Encourage, then, the question: why is mental resilience so monumental in the creative industry? Picture the creative entrepreneur navigating uncharted territories of self-expression while juggling the tangible pressures of market success. Here lies a vibrant but volatile mix, one that calls for mental stamina to maintain equilibrium. Grit, determination, resilience; these are not tangible commodities traded in open markets. Yet, they shape the spirit of entrepreneurship. Picture a resilient mind like an agile dancer; in the face of anxiety's unpredictable rhythm, it doesn't stiffen or panic but adapts and flows, maintaining harmony amidst chaos. It foregoes the roads well-trodden and ventures into the mystery of the unknown, unafraid to experiment, innovate and redefine. Anxiety can shift from a whisper to a roar in these high-stakes, entrepreneurial landscapes. Without proper understanding and management, the unchecked anxiety can burden our creative minds. It is here where we find mental resilience shining the brightest; it is our sanctuary, offering solace and strength, inoculating us against the debilitating weight of unmanaged stress and anxiety.

In these upcoming chapters, we pivot and weave through theory and practice, each page a strategic step towards forging mental resilience. We delve into therapy insights and philosophical reflections to dissect anxiety, dissect our creative blocks, and establish strategies to manage and overcome them. We stand tall in the face of criticism and learn from failure, understanding them as prerequisites for growth rather than symbols of defeat. As we go through these pages together, remember this: beyond the practical wisdom and philosophic contemplation, the heart of this book lies in your hands. It's in your courage to confront your anxieties and your conviction to unlock your innate resilience. You hold the potential for a thriving creative life.

So, let's step forward, dear reader, with empathy and assertiveness, making strides from anxiety to authenticity. Let's immerse ourselves in the art of mental wellbeing and resilience in the creative industry, a vital and oft-undervalued facet that truly separates surviving from thriving in the entrepreneurial journey. The journey may be tumultuous at times, yet rest assured, it is within these tumults we can truly unlock our potential for creative thriving.

Chapter 1: The Creative Mind: Understanding the Unique Mental Health Challenges Faced by the Entrepreneurial Artist

Understanding Anxiety

Anxiety. It's an uninvited guest, waiting patiently to make its presence felt at the most inopportune moments. It's a term we all know, a feeling we all have experienced at some point in our lives. Yet, it remains an elusive and often misunderstood concept, particularly in the context of the creative journey. In its most fundamental form, it's an emotional response to perceived threat or danger. It's a survival mechanism, an evolutionary relic that served our ancestors well in the face of predators or hostile environments. But in our modern world, these 'dangers' often take a more abstract form. They can be deadlines, financial pressures, public speaking engagements or the daunting task of bringing a creative vision to life. The threat is no longer a hungry lion but the fear of failure, rejection, or even success.

In the realm of creative entrepreneurship, this anxiety is not just a fleeting feeling. It's a constant companion, an inherent part of the unique process of creating, innovating, and forging one's path. It's the trepidation that accompanies the blank canvas, the empty page, the silent stage. It's the worry that your ideas are not good enough, the fear that your work won't be accepted or understood, the dread of the unknown future. It's important to understand that anxiety is not inherently negative. It can be a powerful motivator, a spark that ignites creativity, a force that pushes us out of our comfort zones and propels us towards growth and self-discovery. It's a signal, alerting us to the areas in our lives that demand attention and care. But, when anxiety becomes chronic, when it starts to dictate our decisions, cloud our judgement, and hinder our creative process, it becomes a problem.

Understanding anxiety involves recognizing its multifaceted nature. It's more than just a feeling. It's a complex interplay of thoughts, emotions, and physical sensations. It's the racing heart, the sweaty palms, the restless mind. It's the 'what ifs' and 'should haves' that keep us up at night. It's the self-doubt, the imposter syndrome, the perfectionism. It's the nagging feeling that no matter how hard we try, it's never quite enough. But, most importantly, understanding anxiety means acknowledging its presence in our lives. It means looking it in the eye and saying, "I see you. I hear you. I'm ready to learn from you." It's about shifting our perspective, seeing anxiety not as an enemy to be defeated, but as a guide, teaching us a part of ourselves that, when understood and managed, can lead us towards authenticity and creative fulfillment.

Next, we will explore the intricate relationship between creativity and anxiety, examine how anxiety impacts the entrepreneurial journey, and identify personal anxiety triggers. By the end of this chapter, you will have a more comprehensive understanding of anxiety and its role in your creative journey, and you will be better equipped with strategies to manage it effectively. Understanding anxiety is not about eliminating it completely. It's about learning to navigate its turbulent waters, harnessing its energy and channelling it into your creative endeavours. It's about transforming fear into courage, doubt into confidence, and anxiety into authenticity.

The Link Between Creativity and Anxiety

Our creative spirit is a fascinating dance of imagination and innovation, a dynamic interplay that often illuminates the most extraordinary aspects of our personality. But, as we delve deeper into the corridors of creativity, we sometimes stumble upon an unwelcome companion: anxiety. The relationship between creativity and anxiety is a complex one, a tangled web of emotional and cognitive processes that can sometimes feel overwhelming. Creativity, in its essence, is an exploration of the unknown, an endeavour to express the inexpressible. It is the courage to venture into uncharted territories, to bring forth something new and unique. However, this very journey into the unknown can evoke anxiety, as it often involves confronting uncertainty, confronting our deepest fears, and challenging societal norms.

Anxiety, in its simplest form, is a state of unease, a general feeling of worry or fear that can be vague and hard to pin down. It is our body's natural response to perceived danger or threat, a survival mechanism designed to keep us safe. Yet, when this anxiety spills over into our creative process, it can transform from a protective shield into a stifling barrier. The entrepreneurial artist faces a unique set of challenges. The act of creating, of bringing something new into the world, is inherently risky. It requires stepping outside of our comfort zones, exposing ourselves to critique, and grappling with the possibility of failure. This inherent risk can often fuel anxiety, create self-doubt, and lead to creative blocks.

It is essential to remember that anxiety is not an insurmountable obstacle. In many ways, it is a natural part of the creative journey, a sign that we are pushing our boundaries and challenging ourselves. Anxiety, when recognized and properly managed, can even serve as a catalyst for growth, providing valuable insights into our fears and insecurities, and helping us to improve as creative entrepreneurs.

The question then is not how to eradicate anxiety but how to navigate it effectively. How can we harness its energy, transform its power, and use it to fuel our creative endeavours rather than inhibit them? How can we ensure that it sharpens our focus instead of blurring our vision?

Remember, your anxiety does not define you. It is not a measure of your worth or a reflection of your talent. It is simply a part of your journey, a sign that you are pushing your boundaries, challenging your limits, and daring to create. As we venture into the depths of this complex relationship, remember to be gentle with yourself, to treat yourself with kindness and compassion, and to honor the courage it takes to be an entrepreneurial artist.

How Anxiety Affects the Entrepreneurial Journey

Fear, worry, and apprehension are the familiar companions of those who dare to venture into the realm of innovation. It is paramount to understand that anxiety is not merely a psychological nuisance; it is a force that can dramatically shape and steer the course of the entrepreneurial voyage. Anxiety, like an erratic compass, can skew our perception of reality, causing us to oscillate between the extremes of overconfidence and debilitating self-doubt. When anxiety tips the scales, the creative entrepreneur can become paralyzed, ensnared in a cognitive fog that obscures the path to success. The once invigorating pursuit of innovation can morph into a Sisyphean struggle, where each step forward seems to only result in slipping further backward.

In this environment, we may find ourselves shying away from taking calculated risks, opting for safety and predictability. A once vibrant palette of creativity may start to fade, replaced by monotonous hues of comfort and caution. Intrinsic motivation, the lifeblood of the creative entrepreneur, can diminish, sapped by the constant psychological warfare. Anxiety can also rob us of the joy of accomplishment. Even when we do manage to surmount the hurdles and taste success, anxiety can whisper in our ears that it was mere luck, not talent or hard work. A psychological phenomenon prevalent among high-achieving individuals who struggle to internalize their success.

However, it is essential to remember that anxiety can be understood, managed, and even harnessed to energize the search for commercial success. The key lies in acknowledging its presence, understanding its triggers, and developing strategies to keep it in check.

We will explore various therapeutic techniques, philosophical insights, and practical wisdom to arm ourselves. Through this battle, we will discover that anxiety, once tamed, can become an unlikely ally, pushing us towards a deeper understanding of our business profile and orient us to fortifying those areas where we lack. It's also informative to guide us in which partnerships are more like to benefit our creative enterprise.

Identifying Personal Anxiety Triggers

Pause for a moment. Yes, you, with paint on your fingertips or calluses from countless hours spent honing your craft. Pause. Reflect. We thrive amidst the unfettered play of our imagination, yet our innovative minds are often caught in the powerful sway of anxiety. Let's pivot through the door of self-understanding. The first step to manage anxiety effectively is to identify our personal anxiety triggers. By becoming cognizant of what precipitates our anxious thoughts and feelings, we can better strategize our reactions, transforming anxiety from oppressive foe to instructive friend.

So, how does one map the labyrinth of personal triggers? To embark on this introspective journey, consider your entrepreneurial environment. Reflectively, each of us has a unique ecosystem where creativity blossoms—where melodies birth harmonies, where canvas embraces color, where blank pages transform into tales. Yet, within this nourishing milieu lie potential hazards: deadlines that echo like thunderclaps, client expectations that weigh as mountains, or fear of failure that wraps around like a serpent, suffocating creativity. Are these familiar? If so, you have begun to identify triggers that diffuse anxiety throughout your creative landscape. Remember how crucial understanding is on our path from anxiety-inducing confusion to authenticity-inspired clarity. Furthermore, by approaching these triggers with an entrepreneurial mindset —one of problem-solving and innovative thinking— we can devise strategic ways to mitigate their impact, a topic we will explore in depth as we continue our journey.

Past life experience, too, may be an undercurrent shaping your anxiety. Perhaps it's an early failure, a stinging criticism, or societal expectations of 'success.' Ponder these factors; they are lessons from the past manifesting as anxiety in the present. Recall, we are not detectives solving a mystery, but miners in a deep excavation of the self, unearthing the raw stones of experiences, polishing them giftedly to become the jewels of self-understanding. In doing so, we not only illuminate the dark corners of our anxiety but also reclaim the control once seized by the invasive hands of uncertainty. We refashion these triggers into stepping stones, guiding us safely onward in our artistic voyage. Learn these triggers; know them, and you know yourself.

Let this understanding shape your entrepreneurial environment, to build confidence, and to navigate the intricacies of your creative journey with a newfound sense.

The Role of Past Experiences

As we traverse the landscape of our lives, each step we take, each decision we make, leaves a footstep behind. These footsteps are not mere imprints on the soil of our existence, but rather, they are deep, profound trenches that shape our identity, our personality, and most importantly, our mental health. Our past experiences, be they pleasant or painful, formative or forgettable, mold us and leave an indelible mark on our psyche. Creative entrepreneurs, particularly, possess a heightened sensitivity to the impact of their past experiences. Their creativity, their ability to see the world through an innovative lens, is often a product of a suitcase full of their lived experiences. However, this sensitivity can also make them more susceptible to the wounds of past traumas, disappointments, and failures.

The role of past experiences in shaping anxiety is akin to the sculptor who, with each stroke, shapes the raw marble into a work of art. Our past experiences chisel away at the marble of our minds, shaping our fears, anxieties, and worries. They give form to our creative anxieties, and the entrepreneurial environment etches these anxieties deeper into our psyche. Take, for instance, who has experienced repeated rejection in the past. Each rejection, each negative feedback, acts as a hammer blow, chiseling away at their self-confidence, and instilling a deep-seated fear of failure. This fear can then permeate their entrepreneurial courage, leading to anxiety and self-doubt.

However, you will discover that these past experiences, these chiseled marks, are not definitive. They can be softened, reshaped, and even transformed into positive forces. Psychoanalyst Carl Jung once said, "I am not what happened to me, I am what I choose to become."

For now, it is essential to identify and acknowledge the role of past experiences in shaping your creative anxieties. Reflect on your past, map out those experiences that have left a significant mark on you. Recognize that these experiences have shaped your journey so far, but they do not dictate your path forward. Remember, the marble is still in your hands. You have the power to shape, to mold, to create the person you aspire to be. Past experiences are important, but they are just one facet of the multi-dimensional diamond that is you. The entrepreneurial journey is not a straight line; it is a meandering path with twists and turns. Each turn, each twist, is a new opportunity for growth and self-discovery.

In the subsequent chapters, we will explore strategies to manage self-doubt and navigate creative blocks, essential tools for the creative entrepreneur. However, the first step towards managing creative anxieties is understanding them, and understanding begins with reflection. So, take a moment, reflect on your past experiences, and recognize their role in shaping your current anxieties. Remember, reflection is not about dwelling in the past; it is about understanding it, learning from it, and using it as a stepping stone towards a brighter, more authentic future.

The Entrepreneurial Environment

As an entrepreneur, your workspace plays an integral part in your mental health. It is a place that should signify safety, creativity, and productivity. Yet, for the artistic entrepreneur, this space can often morph into a trigger zone - a breeding ground for anxiety. It's essential to understand how the entrepreneurial environment could breed or alleviate anxiety, thus impacting the overall creative process. One must remember that while the world outside contributes to our experiences, it's the world within us that defines our perception of it. It's no secret that our external environment has a direct impact on our internal state, and for creative entrepreneurs, this interplay between the outer and inner world becomes all the more vivid and significant.

Consider your entrepreneurial environment as a microcosm of the broader world. It has its own dynamics, tensions, and potential for growth. Much like how an artist is sensitive to the nuances of shades on a canvas, the entrepreneurial artist is subtly influenced by their surroundings. From the physical structure of the workspace to the emotional climate within teams, every element plays a role in shaping your drive and expectations. Observing therapy's insights, we appreciate that our environment holds power over us only as much as we allow it to. Recognizing and acknowledging the impact of external factors on our mental health is crucial to gaining control over anxiety. In understanding these influences, we empower ourselves to take proactive measures to mitigate triggers and create a supportive environment that fuels our creativity rather than hindering it.

This isn't just about arranging your workspace in a particular way or following a specific routine; it's about crafting an entire ecosystem that is conducive to your mental wellbeing and aligns with your creative spirit. Your entrepreneurial environment stretches beyond physical space. It encompasses your workflow, the nature and quality of your relationships, the stimuli you expose yourself to, the self-imposed demands and deadlines, and so much more. You, as a creative entrepreneur, have the ability to curate your environment and align it with your unique creative rhythm. By doing so, you can transform your entrepreneurial environment from a potential source of anxiety into a sanctuary of inspiration.

Therapeutic Insights on Creative Anxiety

Managed, not eradicated – because let's remember; anxiety is not a pathological symptom to be eradicated, but rather a universal human experience, an integral but challenging part of our human existence.

It was perhaps Yalom, a renowned existential therapist, who considered anxiety not as an interference, but as a confrontation with an existential condition. Yalom's philosophy suggested anxiety could lead us to vital insight about meaning and existence; a concept that skews towards the constructivist school of thought in psychology. Now, I don't mean to dribble off into the depths of psychoanalytic jargon, but cognitive constructivism suggests our knowledge and understanding come from experiencing and interpreting the world. In this regard, the anxiety experienced by the creative entrepreneur can be seen as an opportunity for growth if we can reinterpret and even redefine it.

In fact, many therapists work with people using Cognitive Behavioural Therapy (CBT), which is founded on the redefinition and reframing of thought patterns, particularly those associated with anxiety. CBT offers a unique lens through which creative entrepreneurs may perceive their anxieties as a means of self-exploration, and personal growth. Creativity, by its very nature, is a risk - a leap into the unknown. And where there is risk, there is uncertainty and, therefore, anxiety. As creative entrepreneurs, we paint on a larger canvas. Our risks are not confined to the shadowed corners of a studio; they are center stage, under the spotlight of potential failure or success. Both equally daunting.

The CBT technique of cognitive reframing could be profoundly beneficial for creative entrepreneurs. It involves recognizing negative or distorted thinking patterns and challenging these by considering alternative perspectives. Essentially, you're encouraged to become a philosopher of your thought patterns. An exercise could go like this: when confronted with a trigger, perhaps a negative critique, rather than spiraling into anxiety, you would identify this as distorted cognitions – catastrophizing, perhaps. You would then challenge these thoughts and create an alternative narrative, one that encourages self-compassion and resilience and celebrates the bravery inherent in simply creating.

Another noteworthy psychological model is Mindfulness-Based Cognitive Therapy (MBCT). It's a powerful way of bringing the often unconscious triggers of anxiety to the forefront of our attention. It encourages us to actively acknowledge and accept our anxieties, and in recognizing these thoughts as fleeting rather than defining, we allow ourselves to release them. This acceptance and awareness can be particularly important to the creative entrepreneur. We understand that the birth of creative output comes from within us; there's an intimacy to it that can be both beautiful and terrifying. However, when we remain mindful, we nurture an environment where anxiety can become a catalyst for creativity.

The therapy toolbox is vast and richly varied. Some may find solace in group therapy, sharing experiences and fears with peers. Others might turn to art therapy, using their creativity as a mechanism to navigate anxious feelings – an interesting reframe in itself. As creative entrepreneurs, we are architects of the new and unexplored, and thus an embrace of an innovative approach to managing anxiety is not just beneficial, it is essential. The insights from therapy offer a robust framework through which to understand and harness anxiety.

Self-Care for Creative Entrepreneurs

Self-care, a term frequently bandied about in contemporary conversations, often encased in the sweet allure of spa days and comfort food. This term must bear a richer, deeper significance. More than mere indulgence, self-care for the creative entrepreneur ought to be a strategic endeavour, deliberately crafted to nurture not just the body, but also the mind and spirit. Now, imagine your creativity as a wellspring, bubbling with ideas and innovation. This internal source is precious; it births your dreams and fuels your entrepreneurial journey. However, dredging from this reservoir ceaselessly, without taking time to replenish it, risks leaving it dry and barren. This analogy illustrates the role of self-care for the creative entrepreneur: It is the practice of replenishing your internal wellspring.

Self-care isn't a monolith. It encompasses an array of activities that uplift and rejuvenate you, clearing your mind's clutter so that creativity has room to breathe and flourish. Consequently, self-care practices may vary from person to person. Some might find solace in solitude, nourishing their spirit in silence. They may immerse themselves in nature or lose themselves in the pages of a book. Others may find peace amid the rhythm of their bodies as they dance, exercise, or practice yoga. For many, self-care could also take the form of meditating or embarking on the journey of mindful living.

However, self-care is not simply about indulging in comforting activities. It is also about nurturing internal dialogue. It's about extending grace to oneself, about acknowledging that you, as an artist, are allowed to have days of ebb and flow, allowed to make mistakes, allowed to rest. Reflect on the last time you stumbled on your journey. What was your first instinct? To berate yourself for the misstep, or to extend understanding and patience? Often, we can be our harshest critics and, in those moments, we need to remind ourselves of our humanity: that we are a symphony of successes and failures, each note building towards a unique composition. Moreover, self-care for the creative entrepreneur involves setting boundaries – both personal and professional. It is about recognizing when you need to step back from work or social activities to recharge. It is about stating 'no' when necessary without guilt or justification.

Self-care isn't a journey you have to embark on alone. In fact, sharing your self-care journey with others – be it a trusted friend or a professional therapist – can be extremely beneficial, providing a nurturing dialogue that enhances your understanding of your unique needs. In the end, self-care isn't a luxury for the creative entrepreneur; it's a necessity. It fuels your resilience, fosters mental agility, and creates a protective shield against the common mental health challenges that often accompany the entrepreneurial journey. Embrace self-care as a strategic endeavor, designed to maintain the vibrancy of your creative wellspring. Your creativity is your entrepreneurial lifeblood, your innovative spirit. Protect it. Nurture it. Let it thrive.

Managing Self-Doubt and Imposter Syndrome

Let's start with self-doubt, an intensely intimate, often debilitating experience that is as common as it is idiosyncratic. While it's a universal phenomenon, it tends to grip the creative mind in a unique way. It whispers corrosive affirmations that chip away at your confidence, pushing you toward a vortex of cynicism. It asks daunting questions like, "What if you're not good enough?" or "What if you're simply not cut out for this?"

Imposter syndrome, a psychological term coined by clinical psychologists Pauline Clance and Suzanne Imes in 1978, is an evolution of self-doubt. Here, high-achieving individuals wrestle with an internalized fear of being exposed as a "fraud". Despite evident success, they fail to internalize their accomplishments and persistently credit luck or timing rather than their abilities.

So how do creative entrepreneurs overcome these mental roadblocks? Begin by recognizing that these doubts are a normal part of your journey. It's human to question our adequacy and worth, especially in a field where our creations embody our most intimate selves. Secondly, acknowledge that all your feelings are valid, no matter how irrational they might seem. Is there evidence to support your insecurities? Or are these feelings a product of your mind's habitual worry? A shift in perspective can often unearth the truth beneath the layers of anxiety. Therapeutic insights often emphasize the importance of reframing. Self-doubt can be viewed as an evolutionary tool that urges us to strive for better, to refine our abilities, and to reach out for growth.

Similarly, reframe imposter syndrome as a sign of your humility and the high standards you set for yourself. It means you're not complacent, that you constantly strive to improve and grow. Convert that anxiety into a commitment to learning and professional development. The entrepreneurial journey is a mosaic of failures, successes, questions, and discoveries. Self-doubt and imposter syndrome are crucial pieces of this mosaic, honing your humility and perseverance. The creative journey, although tumultuous, is replete with opportunities for transformation. So, engage with self-doubt, wrestle with the imposter syndrome, but always remember those are symptoms of a healthy relationship with reality.

Overcoming Creative Blocks

Every creative entrepreneur, regardless of their field, knows the stomach-churning frustration of hitting a creative block. You agonize as the cursor blinks mockingly on the blank page, your paintbrush dries while you stare at a pristine canvas, or your guitar gathers dust as you grasp for that elusive melody. Creative blocks are as common as they are a natural part of the innovative process. Yet, when under their suffocating grip, they can feel like personal failures, an indictment on our creative prowess and our worth. Anxiety loves these blocks. It uses them as ammunition, whispering that we're doomed to stagnation, that our well of creativity has finally run dry.

But let's confront anxiety with clarity here: creative blocks are not the death knell of ingenuity or the end of our entrepreneurial journey. Far from it. They are signposts indicating the need to pause, to seek fresh perspectives, and to engage with our creative process more mindfully. Think of your creativity as a river whose flow is interrupted by debris, reducing it to a pained trickle. Your task isn't to berate the river or despair at its diminished flow but to figure out what's causing the blockage and then gently remove it. The river knows its course; it just needs temporary assistance in reclaiming it. Creative energy flows like that river, growing and shrinking as conditions evolve over time.

Identifying the source of the block requires introspection; it demands we venture into our mind's maze. Think back to when the block first appeared. Was there a particular event, a critique, or a challenging client that might have triggered it? Did personal circumstances cast long shadows on your innovative spirits? Understanding the root cause is the first step towards formulating a solution. Nourish your mind and keep it agile by stepping away from your regular workspace. Go on a walk to reconnect with nature or practice mindfulness exercises to harness your wandering thoughts. Temporary diversions can offer spaciousness, enable fresh insights, and allow your thoughts to wander into unexplored pathways, sparking unseen connections.

It's also possible that our block is not about a lack of ideas but about an overwhelming abundance. It's essential to remember that creativity is not about birthing a flawless masterpiece on the first attempt. It's about messy explorations, numerous iterations, and constant growth. Give yourself permission to create without the burden of immediate perfection. Let your ideas breathe and bloom in their time — they are flowers, not assembly line products.

Navigating creative blocks is part introspection, part action. It's about understanding where the obstruction lies and then cultivating an environment that allows your creativity to unfurl again. Creative blocks are not our enemies but our teachers, revealing signposts of our resilience and the extent of our growth. Creativity is no fixed entity. It is an evolving dance between you and your thoughts, a gentle ebb and flow that requires patience, understanding, and introspection. It is in recognizing this flow and fostering an environment to encourage it that we can navigate creative blocks, unfurl our innovative spirits, and continue thriving in our entrepreneurial journey.

Chapter 2: Balancing Work and Personal Life as a Creative Entrepreneur

Creative Work-Life Challenges

Creative entrepreneurship is an alluring journey, enticing with its promise of freedom, independence, and the ability to bring your unique vision to life. But beneath the vibrant hues of this captivating picture lies the blending of work and personal life. This challenge, if not addressed, can lead to undue stress, burnout, and could even stifle the very creativity it intends to foster. Achieving work-life balance as a creative entrepreneur involves a good understanding of the components at play. The process demands attention, patience, and, most importantly, self-awareness.

The challenges of work-life integration in the creative field often stem from blurred boundaries. The same space that fosters your creativity could become an office when you least want it to. Your art might be a source of joy one moment and induce anxiety over executional details the next. It is a common misconception to think of work-life balance as a static state. In reality, it's dynamic. Recognizing this fluid nature is our first step, It prompts us to keep fine-tuning our routines, schedules, and emotional responses. We aren't striving for a perfect equilibrium but rather a harmonious give and take between our personal needs and professional commitments.

Setting boundaries and priorities doesn't mean curtailing our passion or creativity. They aren't walls but rather markers that guide us to a fulfilling and sustainable life. Think of these boundaries as pencil outlines in a sketch, providing structure and direction to the ensuing play of colors. Prioritization is as much about identifying what matters most as it is about learning to let go of the less important. This process can hold different meanings for different individuals and may vary across different stages of life. It's a journey within a journey that calls for retrospection and self-analysis, spearheaded by the question, 'What matters most?'

In the realm of creative entrepreneurship, developing sustainable routines implies embracing a rhythm that catalyzes creativity without exhausting the mind and body. This rhythm shouldn't merely be viewed through the lens of productivity but should cater to overall mental and emotional well-being. Sleep, physical exercise, and recreational activities are not negotiables to be shoved aside when deadlines loom but rather indispensable elements that replenish our creative reservoirs. Research in psychology underscores the restorative power of sleep on cognitive functions, including creativity, which further emphasizes this point.

Nourish your mind with the right blend of rest, work, and leisure activities, pruning away unnecessary stressors and distractions, thus fostering a fertile ground for your creative seeds to flourish.

The balancing act between work and personal life remains a shared quest. Armed with the wisdom from therapy, philosophy, art, and practical insights, let's continue learning, evolving. Remember, it's not about perfect balance, but a meaningful blend that fosters our wellbeing and creativity; after all, we are both the artist and the masterpiece in the making.

Priority Setting & Boundaries

Every artist traversing the labyrinth of creative entrepreneurship is familiar with the overwhelming demands of juggling multiple tasks, projects, roles, and deadlines in a world that never seems to shut down. The whirlwind of duties often engulfs the creative entrepreneur to the point where the line between work and personal life appears blurrier with every passing day. It is at this juncture that we must address the question, "How do we set boundaries and priorities in a line of work that seems to defy traditional definitions of a nine-to-five job?" Defining your priorities is an act of self-awareness and self-fulfillment, a concept that is strongly linked to the authentic self. In the realm of creative entrepreneurship, setting priorities means discerning between what is urgent, what is essential, and what is noise. It demands that we listen keenly to our deepest creativity and defiantly turn our backs on the cacophony of distractions.

Start by asking yourself some reflective questions such as, "What part of my work brings me the most joy, satisfaction, or fulfillment?" "What fuels my creative spirit? What projects are aligned with my long-term vision?" Such introspection paves the way towards a clearer understanding of your authentic self and guides you in channeling your energy efficiently.

Once priorities are set, the next challenge is to establish clear boundaries between work and personal life. The entrepreneurial world often preaches the idea that 'always on' equates to 'always productive.' Yet, this notion is far from the truth. Being 'always on' can lead to unsustainable patterns of work, leading to increase in anxiety, burnout, and weak spots in the psyche that can dampen creativity. Instead, consider adopting a rhythmic approach to life and work that blends active engagement with periods of recovery. This strategy, rooted in the philosophical idea of 'life balance', promotes healthier work habits by integrating moments of solitude and rest into the daily routine. It encourages us to respect the natural cycles of energy, creativity, and productivity by allowing us to be fully present in each activity we undertake.

In practical terms, establishing boundaries might mean reserving certain hours of the day for focused work, while the rest are dedicated to rest, recreation, or relationships. It could also involve setting specific zones in your space for work activities. Such tangible division of time and space serves as a visual and psychological reminder of the need for a balanced life. The key lies in creating a balance that serves your mental health, fuels your creativity, and enables your entrepreneurial journey, rather than restricting it. As we traverse from anxiety to authenticity, taking stock of our priorities, and laying down clear boundaries, aids in crafting a sustainable and fulfilling creative entrepreneurial life. A life that honors our creative spirit while nurturing our mental health and well-being.

Sustainable Well-being Routines

A routine does not imply rigidity. On the contrary, it is the structure that comes from well-established routines that provides us with the freedom and flexibility to nurture our creative spirit. Establishing morning or evening rituals that prioritize self-care, such as meditation, journaling, or even a walk in nature, can lead to increased awareness and mental clarity. In addition to these personal rituals, incorporating practices into your work routine that focus on mental and emotional wellbeing is equally important. Breaks are often overlooked in the entrepreneurial world, with the misconception that constant hustling is the key to success. However, taking short, regular breaks for movement or mindfulness can significantly improve focus, replenish mental energy and foster creativity.

Furthermore, consider incorporating reflective practices into your routine. Time set aside for self-reflection can provide you with insights about your work, your motivation, and the direction you wish to take. This introspection can also shed light on moments of anxiety, enabling you to handle it with wisdom and grace. Undergirding every aspect of these routines for mental and emotional well-being is the concept of self-compassion. Be gentle with yourself as you experiment with different routines. Not every practice will resonate with you, and that's okay. The objective is not perfection but progress towards a work-life rhythm that supports and nourishes your mental and emotional well-being, thereby creating a fertile ground on which your creativity can flourish.

Every creative entrepreneur's rhythm is unique - as unique as the creativity they bring into this world. Embrace your unique rhythm and allow it to guide you in establishing sustainable routines that enhance your mental and emotional well-being, thus fostering a harmonious balance between your work and personal life.

Supportive Networks & Mentors

Every creative entrepreneur needs a support network and mentors who can provide the much-needed guidance through the thorny path of entrepreneurship. Building this network is not, however, an exercise in mass communication, nor is it a frenzy of popularity. It is a thoughtful, strategic process that requires authenticity, empathy, and insight. Many creative entrepreneurs, in their quest for individuality and uniqueness, isolate themselves from others in their field. Understandably, the fear of comparison, the dread of losing originality, or even the anxiety-induced assumption of judgement can fence one in. Sometimes, this isolation only amplifies anxiety. The internal monologue of self-doubt grows louder in the echo chamber of solitude, whereas an engaged dialogue with those around us can refine this internal noise into useful feedback and constructive criticism.

To build a supportive network, creative entrepreneurs need first to understand that every person they encounter holds a unique worldview, a distinct nugget of wisdom, and a different piece of the puzzle they are striving to solve. Networking, then, is not merely about gathering contacts; it is about engaging in meaningful conversations, forging authentic relationships, and valuing intellectual exchange. Approach networking with a perspective of giving rather than receiving. Offer compassion, lend an attentive ear, provide help when needed, and share insights when asked. In this process, you're not only building a supportive network but cultivating your character, fostering your empathy, and broadening your horizon in unimaginable ways.

Mentorship, on the other hand, adds another layer of guidance to this process. A mentor is someone who has toiled through the labyrinth you're about to enter. They are armed with a wealth of experience, further illuminated by the lantern of wisdom. They have battled the same demons of anxiety and self-doubt that currently taunt you, and they've emerged victorious, perhaps battered and worn, yet more resilient than ever. Seek mentors who inspire you. People who represent not just the success you wish to achieve, but also the values you wish to uphold. Remember, the concept of mentorship is not a one-way street. It's not about merely absorbing wisdom passively but actively engaging in the process. Question, debate, reflect, and most importantly, apply what you learn.

Building a supportive network and seeking mentors might seem intimidating, at first. There will be an inherent fear of rejection, a nagging doubt at the back of your mind whether you're good enough. This is where you must hark back to the therapeutic insights we delved into in previous sections, about understanding and managing your anxiety.

Remember, your anxiety is a part of you, but it is not you. It signals you to be cautious, but it does not define your worth or capability. Approach networking and mentorship with a humble open mind, and an unabashed, raw authenticity. You may falter, you may stumble, but every fall will teach you something, every step will take you forward.

Nurturing Connections & Relationships

We often inhabit a domain of constant innovation, relentless commitment, and all-encompassing passion. Yet, within this vibrant landscape lies a risk of isolation, a perilous journey that can often, paradoxically, distance us from meaningful human connection. Here, we pause to remind ourselves, echoing the wisdom of ancient philosophers and contemporary therapists alike, that we are undeniably social beings. The health of our relationships can wield powerful influence on our mental health and wellbeing.

Developing meaningful connections and nurturing relationships do not merely serve as mere adjuncts to our creative journey but are crucial cornerstones of it. They avail us opportunities to share our victories and also equip us with invaluable support in our moments of uncertainty and self-doubt. Aristotle, the philosopher of antiquity, underscored the human predilection for social bonds. He declared man to be a 'social animal,' referring to our inbuilt disposition for companionship and friendship. it's essential to remember this fundamental aspect of our humanity. We are not islands; we enjoy benefits from the rich diversity of socio-emotional nutrients that healthy relationships offer. Input from colleagues, family, and friends doesn't only sustain us emotionally but can also become a rich wellspring from which new creative ideas emerge. A dialogue that sparks a new thought, a casual remark leading to an insightful realization, or constructive feedback that catalyzes improvement in our work—all these treasures are intrinsic to the relational realm.

So how do we cultivate these relationships in our increasingly busy, entrepreneurial lives? Intentionality is key. Intentionality, the deliberate act of carving out time for relationships, of showing genuine interest in the lives of those around us, can shift our perspective and enrich our work. Simply put, it's about being present. When we engage with others, are we fully there, in the moment, devoid of distractions? Or does our multi-tasking entrepreneurial mind hinder us from genuinely connecting? Being present, both physically and emotionally, is an art that requires conscious effort but yields profound rewards. The quality of our connections often mirrors the genuineness of our engagement. Engaging authentically, demonstrating vulnerability, and expressing empathy can catalyze strong bonds that can both enrich our personal lives and foster a supportive work environment.

The American author Kurt Vonnegut, known for his satirical literary style, once held a fascinating conversation with his son regarding his profession. When asked what he did for a living, Vonnegut responded, "I tell stories, would you like to hear one?" This seemingly simple exchange encapsulates the essence of nurturing relationships—an eagerness to share our stories and an equal curiosity to hear others'. Continue to pour your energy into your work, but also remember to nurture the relationships that give color to your canvas. These meaningful connections enrich not only our personal lives but our creative spirit, infusing our entrepreneurial journey with warmth, wisdom, and perspective.

Moments of introspection and solitude are necessary and valuable to process and reflect. Nevertheless, an excessive emphasis on solitary artistic endeavor can evoke a sense of disconnection, contributing to anxiety and potentially other mental health concerns. The philosophy here is straightforward: seek genuine connections, embrace authenticity, prioritize presence, and remember that the creative process is as much about engaging with the world around us as it is about exploring the world within us.

Chapter 3: Balancing Passion and Practicality in the Creative Journey

Exploring the Balance of Artistic Passion and Practicality

There exists a deep tension between the heart's longing and the world's demands. Artistic passion, the fire that fuels the creative spirit, is a powerful force. It is the spark that ignites the imagination, the drive that propels us to create, to innovate, to push boundaries. It is the wellspring of our most profound and transformative ideas. It is the essence of who we are as artists and entrepreneurs. Yet, we live in a world of practical considerations. A world where art must not only inspire but also sell. A world where creativity must be balanced with commerce, where the artist's vision must meet the market's demand. This world, with its realities and constraints, can often feel at odds with our artistic passion.

How does one navigate this dance? How does one balance the heart's longing with the world's demands? How does one reconcile the artist's vision with the market's needs?

The first step is to acknowledge this tension. To recognize that it is a natural part of the creative entrepreneurial journey. This tension is not a sign of failure or inadequacy. Rather, it is a testament to the complexity and richness of the creative process. It is a reflection of the multifaceted nature of our roles as creative entrepreneurs.

The second step is to embrace this tension. To see it not as a hindrance but as an opportunity. An opportunity for innovation. This tension, when approached with curiosity and openness, can lead to new insights, new ideas, new possibilities. It can push us to explore uncharted territories, to challenge our assumptions, to redefine our boundaries.

The third step is to navigate this tension. To find a path that honors both our artistic passion and the practical realities of our work. This path, while unique to each of us, often involves a process of negotiation. A process of give and take, of compromise and adjustment. It involves making choices, setting priorities, and making sacrifices. It involves learning to balance our desire for artistic freedom with our need for financial stability.

It can be challenging, frustrating, even painful at times. But it is also rewarding, and ultimately, transformative. To balance our dreams with our realities, to create art that is not only meaningful to us but also valuable to others. Our artistic passion and the practical realities of our work are not opposing forces but complementary aspects of our creative journey.

Finding and Sustaining Inspiration

If your business depends on creativity, inspiration is not a mere luxury; it is the lifeblood that fuels our endeavours. Yet, it is often elusive, a fleeting wisp of an idea that can vanish as quickly as it appeared. So, how do we find and maintain this elusive entity?

First, understand that inspiration is not a passive process. It is not something that simply happens to us, but rather, it is something we actively seek out and cultivate. Our internal world and the external environment, a symbiotic relationship that requires both receptivity and action. To find inspiration, we must first be open to it. This means cultivating a mindset of curiosity and wonder, a willingness to explore and experiment. It means stepping outside our comfort zones, embracing the unfamiliar, and challenging our preconceived notions. It means being receptive to the world around us, to the beauty and complexity of life in all its forms. We must also actively seek it out. This can take many forms, from immersing ourselves in nature or art, to engaging with diverse cultures and perspectives, to simply taking time for quiet reflection and introspection. The key is to engage with the world in a way that feeds our creative spirit, that stimulates our imagination and fuels our passion.

Maintaining inspiration, on the other hand, requires a different set of strategies. It involves creating a conducive environment for creativity, one that nurtures our artistic spirit and facilitates the flow of ideas. This could mean designing a workspace that sparks creativity, establishing routines that foster focus and productivity, or surrounding ourselves with people who inspire and challenge us. It also involves taking care of our mental and emotional well-being. Just as a plant needs water and sunlight to thrive, our creative spirit needs nourishment and care. This means practicing self-care, managing stress, and seeking support when needed. It means honoring our emotions, embracing our unique creative process, and giving ourselves permission to rest and recharge.

But perhaps the most important aspect of maintaining inspiration is cultivating a deep and enduring love for our craft. This love, this passion, is what will sustain us through the inevitable ups and downs of the creative journey. It is what will keep us going when inspiration seems scarce, when the path ahead seems uncertain. It is, in essence, the fuel that keeps our creative fires burning.

Therapy in Decision-Making

As we find ourselves at the crossroads of passion and practicality, our hearts pull us towards the allure of our artistic pursuits, while our minds remind us of the pragmatic realities of life. This dichotomy can lead to a state of mental turmoil, often resulting in anxiety and indecision. It is here that therapeutic approaches can provide a beacon of clarity. Therapy, in its essence, is a process of introspection, self-awareness, and growth. It encourages us to delve deep into our psyche, understand our motivations, and confront our fears. This introspective journey can be instrumental in making decisions that align with both our passion and practicality.

One therapeutic approach that can be particularly beneficial is Cognitive Behavioral Therapy (CBT). CBT is a form of psychotherapy that challenges and changes unhelpful cognitive distortions and behaviors, improves emotional regulation, and develops personal coping strategies. It encourages us to question our automatic thoughts, assumptions, and beliefs, thereby enabling us to make more informed and rational decisions.

Let's consider a common scenario faced by many creative entrepreneurs: the decision to leave a stable job to pursue a creative passion. The thought of leaving the security of a regular income can trigger a cascade of negative thoughts and fears. "What if I fail? What if I can't pay my bills? What if people judge me?" These automatic thoughts can paralyze us, preventing us from taking the leap towards our dreams. CBT encourages us to challenge these automatic thoughts. Is failure certain? Are there no other means to pay bills? Will people's judgment truly impact our happiness and success? By questioning these beliefs, we can often find that they are not as absolute or terrifying as we initially thought. This process can help us make a more balanced decision, one that considers both our passion for creativity and our practical needs.

Another therapeutic approach that can aid in decision-making is Mindfulness-Based Cognitive Therapy (MBCT). MBCT combines mindfulness strategies with elements of CBT. Mindfulness encourages us to be fully present in the moment, to observe our thoughts and feelings without judgment. This heightened awareness can provide valuable insights into our true desires and fears, thereby guiding our decisions. For instance, if we find ourselves constantly daydreaming about painting during our 9-to-5 job, it might indicate a deep-seated passion for art. On the other hand, if the thought of financial instability sends us into a panic, it might suggest a need for financial security. By being mindful of these thoughts and emotions, we can make decisions that honor both our passion and our practical needs.

Therapeutic approaches, such as CBT and MBCT, provide us with the tools to navigate the complex terrain of passion and practicality. They encourage us to challenge our fears, understand our desires, and make decisions that align with our authentic selves. By integrating these therapeutic approaches into our decision-making process, we can create a harmonious balance between our creative passions and practical considerations, thereby fostering a sense of fulfillment and wellbeing in our entrepreneurial journey.

Reflections on Finding Harmony Between Passion and Practicality

As we delve into the philosophical realm, we find that this balance isn't just a struggle faced by the modern entrepreneur. It's a timeless question that has been pondered by philosophers for centuries. The ancient Greeks, for example, placed great importance on the concept of 'Eudaimonia', a term that translates to 'flourishing' or 'the good life'. This encompasses more than mere happiness; it involves fulfilling one's potential and living in accordance with one's true nature. In the context of the creative entrepreneur, Eudaimonia can be seen as the harmonious union of passion and practicality. It is about aligning our creative pursuits with our practical needs. It's about finding that sweet spot where our passion fuels us, and our practicality grounds us. It's about being true to ourselves, while also being mindful of the world around us.

How do we ensure that our passion doesn't consume us, leaving us lost in a sea of impractical dreams? Or that our practicality doesn't suffocate our creativity, leaving us feeling unfulfilled and uninspired? The key lies in self-awareness. It lies in knowing ourselves deeply, understanding our strengths and weaknesses, our desires and fears. It requires us to be honest with ourselves, to confront our realities, and to make conscious choices that align with our authentic selves.

This self-awareness allows us to harness our passion, to channel it into our creative pursuits without it consuming us. It allows us to acknowledge our practical needs, to make decisions that ensure our survival and wellbeing without stifling our creativity. We must remember that passion and practicality are not opposing forces. They are two sides of the same force which can lead to a fulfilling and sustainable creative journey. So, as we continue, let us strive for Eudaimonia. Let us strive for us to flourish, to fulfill our potential, and to live in accordance with our true nature.

Chapter 4: The Rollo May Approach: Building a Foundation for Self-Determination

Rollo May: Existential Anxiety, Creativity & Artistic Entrepreneurship

In the annals of psychological theory, few voices have been as influential and as relevant to the creative entrepreneur as that of Rollo May. An American existential psychologist, May's work offers a profound exploration of the human condition. His theories, rooted in philosophy, provide a roadmap for understanding the unique challenges faced by creative entrepreneurs and offer pathways towards self-determination and authenticity. May's work centers around the concept of existential anxiety, a term that refers to the inherent unease we experience as we grapple with our existence's fundamental uncertainties. This existential anxiety is more than just a source of discomfort; it is an essential catalyst for creativity, pushing us to confront our limitations and seek new ways of understanding and engaging with the world.

For the creative entrepreneur, this existential anxiety can be both a source of inspiration and a debilitating burden. On one hand, it drives the relentless pursuit of innovation, the creation of something new and meaningful in an uncertain world. On the other hand, it can lead to feelings of isolation, self-doubt, and paralyzing fear of failure. May's perspective on this anxiety is not one of eradication but of acceptance and integration. He believed that by acknowledging and embracing our existential anxieties, we could harness them as a transformative force, driving us towards self-actualization and authentic creative expression. In his words, "Anxiety is essential to the creative process...The courage to create is born out of the confrontation with anxiety."

This is not to say that the process is easy. Confronting existential anxiety requires courage, self-awareness, and a willingness to grapple with the fundamental uncertainties of existence. It involves a journey into the heart of our fears, our dreams, our passions, and our deepest selves. It is a journey that demands vulnerability, tenacity, and an unwavering commitment to authenticity.

For those willing to embark on this journey, the rewards can be profound. By embracing their existential anxieties, creative entrepreneurs can unlock new levels of creativity, resilience, and authenticity. They can build a foundation for self-determination, defining their paths not by societal expectations or external metrics of success, but by their deepest passions and values. They can transform their anxieties into a potent force for innovation, creating not just successful businesses, but meaningful lives. The Rollo May approach to existential anxiety offers a roadmap for this journey. It is an invitation to embrace the full spectrum of our human experience, harnessing our anxieties as a catalyst for authentic creative expression and entrepreneurial success.

Empowering creative entrepreneurs to define their paths independently.

Rollo May emphasized the significance of self-determination in his works. He believed in the power of an individual to create their own destiny. This principle is particularly relevant to the entrepreneurial artist, who is tasked not only with producing unique and compelling work but also with navigating the business world.

When we talk about defining our path independently, we are talking about more than just setting goals and making plans. It is about asserting our autonomy, embracing our individuality, and acknowledging our inherent worth. It is about defying societal expectations that may not align with our values and aspirations. It is about making decisions that resonate with our authentic selves, even when they may seem unconventional or risky. We often find ourselves in environments that are rife with competition and comparison. We are constantly bombarded with images of success that may not reflect our personal definition of achievement. It is easy to fall into the trap of trying to emulate others' paths, losing sight of our unique journey in the process. However, it is crucial to remember that no two journeys are the same, and there is no one-size-fits-all formula for success.

May's existential philosophy encourages us to embrace our individuality and to acknowledge that our path is ours alone to forge. Understanding that our experiences, our perspectives, and our creative processes are unique and valuable. Recognizing that our journey, with all its twists and turns, is not just a means to an end but a meaningful and enriching process in itself. Embracing this philosophy can free us from the shackles of societal expectations and allow us to explore uncharted territories with courage, curiosity and make decisions that align with our core values and aspirations.

Techniques to Break Free from Societal Expectations

The societal expectations that we are often bombarded with can be a heavy burden. It may seem as if there are predetermined paths you are expected to follow, a set of rules you must abide by, or a certain image you must project. This pressure can stifle creativity and authenticity, two cornerstones upon which a successful creative venture is built. Rollo May urged us to break free from such expectations. He believed that we must courageously embrace our freedom and take responsibility for our own existence. It is this existential courage that empowers us to define our paths independently, an approach that is particularly applicable to the life of an artistic entrepreneur.

But, how can we break free from societal expectations? Here are some techniques that integrate May's philosophy with psychological insights and practical wisdom.

Firstly, we must recognize the influence of societal expectations. They often operate under the surface, subtly shaping our thoughts and actions. Reflect on your decisions and ask yourself: Are these truly my desires or am I succumbing to external pressure? This self-awareness is the first step towards emancipation.

Secondly, embrace your unique identity. Each of us has a distinct blend of experiences, talents, and perspectives. This uniqueness should not be suppressed. Your unique voice is your greatest asset as a creative entrepreneur. Do not dilute it to fit into a predefined mold.

Thirdly, cultivate courage. Breaking free from societal expectations requires boldness. You might face criticism or misunderstanding, but remember that your journey is not about pleasing others. It is about expressing your authentic self and creating meaningful work.

Lastly, take responsibility for your life. Understand that you are the architect of your own destiny. When you stop attributing your life's course to societal expectations, you reclaim your power. You begin to steer your life in the direction that resonates with your true self.

Breaking free from societal expectations is not an act of rebellion but an act of authenticity. It is about staying true to our visions, even when they do not align with the mainstream. This is the path to a fulfilling and successful creative venture.

Practical Tips to Harnessing Struggle for Creative Expression

As the sun rises, so does it set; as the tide ebbs, so does it flow. The natural world is governed by an intrinsic rhythm, an equilibrium of opposition and reconciliation. It is this duality that breathes life into existence, something that we must learn to emulate within our own lives.

Struggle and ease, failure and success, anxiety and tranquility, these are the rhythms that imbue our creative journey with depth and richness. It is through the struggle that we find our most authentic selves and our most profound expressions of creativity. This is not a novel concept, but a universal truth echoed in the wisdom of philosophers, therapists, and artists alike. The struggle is not an aberration to be avoided but an essential stepping stone towards creative expression. It is the grit within the oyster that gives birth to the pearl. Our struggles, our anxieties, our failures — these are not roadblocks on our journey but the very material with which we sculpt our creative destinies.

Rollo May understood this intimately. He recognized the inherent struggle in the creative process and posited that it was not merely a by-product of creativity, but rather its lifeblood. He asserted, "Creativity arises out of the tension between spontaneity and limitations, the latter (like the river banks) forcing the spontaneity into the various forms which are essential to the work of art or poem." Our struggles, our limitations, they act as the river banks, guiding our creative energies into unique expressions of art and entrepreneurship. They are not to be feared or shunned but embraced and utilized as tools for creative innovation.

So how do we harness this wisdom in a practical sense? How do we transform our struggles into the fuel for our creative fires? We must acknowledge our struggles. Denial or avoidance only serves to stifle our creative potential. By acknowledging our anxieties, our doubts, our fears, we validate our experiences and create the space necessary for transformation. We must learn to sit with our struggles. This is not a passive act but an active engagement with our challenges. It involves introspection, contemplation, and a willingness to delve into the depths of our discomfort. This is where therapy can be a valuable companion, providing us with the tools to navigate these murky waters. We must channel our struggles into our creative work. This is where the magic happens. Our struggles become the themes of our art, the lessons in our stories, the ethos of our entrepreneurial ventures. They become the unique selling points that differentiate us from the crowd, the authentic voice that resonates with others who share similar struggles.

Struggle is not the enemy of the creative entrepreneur. It is our teacher, our muse, our catalyst for growth. It is the crucible in which we forge our creative identities and cultivate our unique contributions to the world. So let us not shy away from the struggle but rather embrace it, for it is in the struggle that we find our most authentic and profound creative expression.

Chapter 5: Redefining Success: the Philosophical Shift

Philosophical Insights on Redefining Success in the Creative Realm

For many, success is a tangible concept—monetary gain, accolades, public recognition, a robust social media following. However, for the creative entrepreneur, sculpting an authentic definition of success can be an entirely different undertaking and a journey in itself.

When we look to philosophy, the wellspring of wisdom where we can probe the nature of accomplishment and fulfillment. In the words of French philosopher René Descartes, "It is not enough to have a good mind; the main thing is to use it well." This sentiment serves as a compelling starting point for our exploration. For the creative entrepreneur, it's not sufficient to possess talent or vision; their authentic success lies in their ability to apply these gifts in meaningful and fulfilling ways. Descartes compels us to question the value we place on our abilities, not by society's measures, but by how we use them to enrich our lives and the lives of others.

Aristotle, one of the great figures of Greek philosophy, argued that true happiness is found in a life lived for its own sake—where we are actualizing our potential and realizing our unique purpose. Thus, 'Eudaimonia' becomes an expression of personal success that transcends traditional metrics. To transpose this philosophy into the creative realm, consider your artistry or entrepreneurial endeavor as an extension of your being. In this light, success becomes less about external validation and more about your personal growth, your ability to express your unique vision, and the fulfillment that springs from living your purpose authentically.

Take a moment to reflect on your creative journey so far. What have been the moments that ignited a sense of fulfillment or satisfaction? How have these moments been linked to your personal growth and self-expression? Understanding this, we can start to align our measures of success with our authentic selves. Instead of seeking validation from external sources, we learn to value our journey, our growth, and the unique paths we carve in the world.

Philosopher Friedrich Nietzsche once declared, "That which does not kill us makes us stronger." We can derive strength and resilience from our failures, viewing them not as stumbling blocks but as stepping stones to our unique version of success. In fact, they become proof of our courage to live authentically and pursue our passions.

In the end, the philosophical shift to redefine success asks us to honor our journey, echoing the sentiment of Ralph Waldo Emerson: "Life is a journey, not a destination." The transformative act of redefining success thus becomes about valuing the process over the endpoint, the becoming over the being.

As you reflect on these insights, consider how you might reshape your personal definition of success in the creative realm. Remember, it's not about the world's validation but about your growth, resiliency, and the authenticity of your creative journey. In this light, every step forward—no matter how small—becomes a testament to your unique kind of success.

Encouraging a Shift from External Validation to Intrinsic Fulfillment

The allure of external validation can be a potent motivator. The applause after a successful performance, the glowing reviews following a book launch, or the beaming pride in a mentor's eyes can be intoxicating. External validation, however, is a two-edged sword. It can fuel our ambitions, yes, but it can also chain us to the unpredictable whims of an ever-changing audience. It is crucial to understand that seeking external validation is not inherently wrong. It is, after all, a fundamental aspect of our human nature - the desire for acceptance, appreciation, and acknowledgment from others. However, herein lies the grand paradox of external validation: the very people whose approval we seek are just like us - they are fallible, they have biases, and they have limited perspectives. They are not absolute judges of our worth, and their opinions should not be the singular determinant of our sense of success.

The antidote? A shift towards **intrinsic fulfillment**.

Intrinsic fulfillment emanates from within, independent of external accolades and critiques. It is the gratification derived from creating art that brings us joy, from engaging in work that aligns with our values, from marching to the beat of our own drum. Intrinsic fulfillment is the fulfillment of self, not others. It's about mapping out one's unique definition of success and striving for it with unwavering tenacity. This shift from external validation to intrinsic fulfillment requires a profound self-awareness, an audacious self-belief, and a relentless self-commitment - qualities that are cultivated over time. But this shift is more than a mere mindset adjustment; it is a philosophical realignment of our life compass.

The journey to intrinsic fulfillment begins by asking ourselves introspective questions: What truly brings me joy? Whose opinions have I been prioritizing, and why? What would success look like if I defined it on my own terms? As artists, it is easy to become captives of the court of public opinion. We often mistake the applause of the crowd for the success we seek. But remember, applause is ephemeral; it begins and ends. Your personal fulfillment, however, can be lasting. This shift requires courage as It involves embracing the risk of displeasing the crowd, the possibility of dissenting voices, the likelihood of traversing a path less trodden. It involves trading the fleeting comfort of conformity for the enduring satisfaction of authenticity.

Intrinsic fulfillment means creating art that resonates with your soul, even if it does not conform to current trends. It's about building a business that reflects your values, even if it means turning down opportunities that don't align with them. The shift from external validation to intrinsic fulfillment is about finding your own rhythm in the cacophony of others' expectations. It's about understanding that your work's worth is not determined solely by its popularity but by the passion, authenticity, and dedication infused into it. Those are accomplishments in their own that can keep us motivated to continuing pursuing the next peak in our commercial journey.

Intrinsic fulfillment is not about rejecting the world outside; rather, it is about embracing the world within you. It's about understanding that you are not merely a mirror reflecting others' opinions but a light, emanating your unique radiance. The journey from external validation to intrinsic fulfillment is not easy, but it is profoundly rewarding. It is a journey that liberates us from the shackles of others' expectations and allows us to explore the expansive landscapes of our creative potential.

Authentic Goal-Setting Strategies

To set authentic and personally meaningful goals, we need to first understand our own intricate and evolving definition of success. Through a process of reflective contemplation, we begin by asking ourselves: What does success look like to me? This question is not about the tangible trophies of achievement but rather the intangible fulfilment that bubbles up from our very core. This is a process of self-discovery and it demands courage - the courage to question, to challenge, to diverge.

The entrepreneur who seeks authenticity must learn to listen to their own inner narrative, to the hum of their intuition and the rhythm of their passion. Setting authentic goals involves peeling back layers of societal expectations, of preconceived notions, and external pressures. It requires us to redefine success on our own terms and according to our own values. Instead of solely chasing growth and profit, we might choose to prioritize creativity, innovation, personal development, or meaningful contribution.

Just as art is not measured by the price at which it sells but by the emotion it invokes and the thoughts it provokes, authentic goals are not solely centered around conspicuous achievements. Once we've identified these goals, it's essential to embed them into our entrepreneurial journey. Each step towards an authentic goal is a step towards a deeper connection with our work, with our art, with ourselves.

Chapter 6: Overcoming Obstacles and Persevering in the Creative Field

Developing Resilience and Persistence

Usually, we are not just facing the usual challenges of establishing a business, but also the nuanced complexities of the creative realm. This ability is aptly termed 'resilience', a cornerstone for survival and success in the creative field. Resilience is the psychological strength that enables you to bounce back from adversity. It is a mental muscle that can be cultivated and strengthened with conscious effort and practice. Resilience isn't just about enduring hardship but using that hardship as a springboard for growth and innovation. It's about transforming the adversity into a tool of progress, a catalyst propelling you towards your entrepreneurial goals. It fuels your persistence, that relentless pursuit of your creative vision.

It's no secret that the creative journey is fraught with rejection, criticism, and daunting challenges. Picasso, a figurehead of 20th-century art, once noted that "Every act of creation is first an act of destruction". In other words, the path to creativity often involves deconstructing old patterns, ideas, and even parts of ourselves. This process can be unsettling, even painful at times. However, it is through this destruction, through these obstacles and hardships, that we find an opportunity for profound growth and new creation. Developing resilience is an intentional process, a psychological expedition that requires self-awareness, emotional intelligence, and a strong support network. It begins with cultivating a mindset that views challenges not as insurmountable threats but as opportunities for growth. Every obstacle you encounter on your journey is a chance to learn and improve. When you fail, you gather valuable insights that can guide your future endeavors. This mindset shift is the first step towards developing resilience.

Psychological studies have shown that maintaining a positive outlook and practicing optimism are valuable in building resilience. This doesn't mean you should ignore your problems or pretend that everything is perfect. Instead, acknowledging the challenges yet focusing on the potential opportunities they present, finding the silver lining amidst a storm, the rainbow after a downpour.

Another crucial factor in resilience building is self-care. As a creative entrepreneur, it's easy to fall into the trap of overworking, neglecting your physical, emotional, and mental well-being in the pursuit of your entrepreneurial dreams. Overwork and burnout can deplete your resilience reserves, leaving you ill-equipped to handle challenges. Therefore, self-care, setting healthy boundaries, and maintaining work-life balance are essential in maintaining and enhancing your resilience. Equally important is the role of a strong support network in nurturing resilience. The entrepreneurial journey can be a lonely one, especially in the creative field where your work is often a deeply personal reflection of yourself. Having a reliable support network- be it family, friends, mentors, or like-minded entrepreneurs, can provide emotional support, constructive feedback, and valuable insights that can help you endure and overcome challenges.

Resilience is not innate or static. It's a dynamic quality that evolves and strengthens with experience, practice, and self-awareness. Cultivate resilience, embrace each obstacle as a stepping stone, each failure and setback as a learning opportunity to fuel your creative fire, guiding you through the highs and lows of your creative journey. Your ability to bounce back from adversity, to learn, adapt, and grow from challenges, is your greatest asset as a creative entrepreneur. Embrace resilience, and you embrace your capacity to persevere and thrive in the creative field.

Embracing Adaptability in the Creative Industry

Within the creative landscape, the tides of change are both inevitable and unpredictable. They bring with them new challenges, novel opportunities, and sometimes, unsettling uncertainties. As the insightful philosopher Heraclitus stated, "Change is the only constant in life." Understanding this timeless wisdom is key in developing a healthy relationship with change and fostering adaptability. Our ability to adapt is a testament to the incredible resilience inherent in the human spirit. And it is this resilience that fuels our journey through the oscillating highs and lows of the creative process. One day you might be reveling in the euphoria of a completed project, the next you might find yourself grappling with a new challenge that upends everything.

Adaptability is not about discarding your authentic creative vision or altering your core values. Rather, it's about being open to new perspectives, willing to refine your approach, and ready to seize opportunities as they arise. Cultivating an entrepreneurial mindset that thrives on innovation and isn't deterred by the unfamiliar.

But how does one cultivate such adaptability? Acknowledging and accepting change as an integral part of the creative process. Instead of perceiving change as an adversary, frame it as a catalyst for evolution and innovation. Remember, every transition is an invitation to learn, grow, and create anew. In the face of change, trust your ability to navigate through unchartered territories, and know that even if you falter, you possess the resilience to rise again.

Adaptability also involves the capacity to make strategic decisions under changing circumstances. This calls for a blend of intuition and analytical reasoning, an entrepreneurial balancing act, if you will. Be willing to pivot when necessary, but never lose sight of your overarching creative vision. Cultivate a hunger for learning, a desire to explore, and an openness to diverse perspectives. Encourage a mindset that thrives on questions rather than fearing them. As the philosopher Bertrand Russell once asserted, "In all affairs, it's a healthy thing now and then to hang a question mark on the things you take for granted."

Celebrating Successes and Personal Growth

We often find ourselves entwined in a relentless pursuit for success. This pursuit, if left unchecked, can transform into an unending chase, where the finish line keeps shifting farther away. The issue lies in the perception and definition of success; if it is seen as an elusive, distant destination, then we tend to belittle our immediate accomplishments and undervalue our personal growth. Success is not an idyllic paradise waiting at the end of the entrepreneurial journey; it's the countless moments of triumph and learning along the way. It's about appreciating our progress, even if it's minute or slow.

Consider each accomplishment, whether it's completing a project, receiving positive feedback, or even overcoming a creative block, as a mini-success. By doing so, you start to shift your focus from the overwhelming pressure of the ultimate goal to finding fulfillment in the journey itself. This approach not only reduces anxiety but also fosters a sense of self-efficacy which is integral to building resilience. The beauty of this perspective is that it allows us to recognize and value our personal growth. Entrepreneurship, especially within the creative field, is as much a process of self-discovery as it is of building a thriving business. It allows you to uncover latent talents, explore new ideas, and refine your skills.

As you navigate through your story, remember to pause, appreciate, and celebrate your wins. By doing so, you are not just boosting your morale but also reinforcing the belief in your capabilities. It's a gentle reminder to yourself that you have come a long way and are capable of traversing the path ahead. In your relentless pursuit of grand success, do not forget to celebrate the now. Let's not lose sight of the beautiful mosaic of victories and lessons that constitute our journey. For, as much as success is about reaching our goals, it's also about appreciating the journey and acknowledging how far we've come.

Chapter 7: Handling Criticism and Rejection

Philosophical Exploration of Rejection and Failure

As artists, we stand at this frontier, fraught with the possibility of rejection, our visions often colliding with the expectations and tastes of an audience we seek to charm.

In the raw vulnerability of our artistic offerings, philosophical questions about rejection and failure emerge. What is the essence of rejection? Is failure an indelible stain upon our character, or might it be a crucible for profound growth? Rejection, when dissected through the lens of philosophy transcends its immediate sting, inviting to contemplate our relationship with our work and the world. Socrates' famed maxim, "Know thyself," resonates. To understand rejection, we must first understand ourselves—our values, our purpose. Failure, too. It is an existential puzzle, prodding us to dig into the roots of our creative intention. Does our work truly express something relevant about our experience, or are we merely chasing ephemeral applause? When brushed by the wings of failure, we must consider whether we are being guided by an authentic inner compass or lost in a maze of external expectations.

We, as entrepreneurs, are tasked with navigating these philosophical conundrums, knowing full well that the marketplace is neither a philosopher nor a therapist. It judges swiftly and without mercy. It is within this very crucible that we are given the opportunity to refine our artistry and fortify our journey. While the pain of rejection is universal, its impact is deeply personal. Each of us grapples with it in the quiet chambers of our own psyche, contending with the whisperings of self-doubt that accompany every 'no'. But as we peel back the layers of discomfort, we unearth insights that can become the bedrock upon which we rebuild our creative endeavors.

It is in these instances that wisdom from the stoic philosophers offers solace. Marcus Aurelius reminded us that we have power over our mind—not outside events. Realize this, and you will find strength. When facing rejection, we can choose to see it not as a reflection of our worth but as a non offensive event—a simple mismatch between what is offered and what is sought. This approach sometimes requires a level of detachment from our work, recognizing it as an extension of ourselves but not the sum total of our value. It requires that we step back and reassess not just what was rejected but why. Was it the style, the timing, or perhaps the audience itself? In understanding the 'why,' we lay the groundwork for enriching our possible destination.

Criticism and rejection are inextricable from the creative process. They are but waypoints—challenging, yes, but also illuminating. Through them, we come to know resilience not just as a concept, but as a lived experience—one that shapes us into more nuanced creators and more empathetic human beings.

Coping Mechanisms for Handling Criticism and Rejection

Our artistic expressions are extensions of our innermost thoughts and feelings, thus making any external critique feel deeply personal. While it's a universal truth that criticism—constructive or otherwise—can serve as a potent catalyst for growth, the sting of rejection has a way of eclipsing that silver lining. It is in these moments where our mental fortitude is tested. The key lies not in erecting an impenetrable facade but in developing a philosophical and therapeutic understanding of the nature of criticism and rejection. Reframe your perspective. Criticism, especially when offered constructively, is not an attack, but rather an invitation to view our work through a different lens, to challenge our preconceptions, and to expand beyond the confines of our current capabilities. The artistry within us thrives when exposed to diverse viewpoints, even when they seem at odds with our own vision.

To navigate rejection, draw upon the wellspring of self-compassion. Remember, your worth is not determined by the acceptance or critique of others. In the therapy room, we explore the concept of 'self-talk'—the silent conversation we have with ourselves. It's imperative that this self-talk be kind, forgiving, and nurturing. When we internalize a benevolent voice, we become our own source of comfort and encouragement. Another coping mechanism that has proven its efficacy time and again is the practice of detachment. This is not to be misconstrued as a lack of care or investment in one's work. Rather, it is the ability to separate one's self-worth from the work itself. We must strive to acknowledge that our creations can be imperfect or subject to critique without diminishing our value as a creator or as a person.

Maintaining a growth mindset is also pivotal. When faced with criticism, ask yourself: What can I learn from this? Embrace the fact that you are a work in progress, and every rejection is but a step on the staircase towards improvement. Remember the potential for the therapeutic power of community. Being surrounded by fellow creative minds who speak the language of passion and perseverance creates a safety net and echoes of inspiration. Peer groups, mentors, and trusted colleagues can offer their insight, share their own stories of overcoming barriers, and remind us that our experiences are part of a shared human condition.

Additionally, it is crucial to establish and maintain a reflective practice—meditative contemplation, or artistic outlets that allow for the processing of emotions associated with critique. In this private space, free from the eyes of the world, we can dissect our reactions, identify patterns of thought that may not serve us, and strategize on how to approach similar situations in the future with a fortified heart. Be ready to unleash artistic courage—the willingness to be vulnerable again despite past rejections. Each time you put forth your work, you demonstrate an admirable defiance against the fear of criticism. This audaciousness is at the core of what it means to be a creative entrepreneur.

Principles for Maintaining Confidence and Self-Worth

Essentially, understand that the value of your work—and indeed, your value as a creator—is not solely determined by the acceptance or approval of others. The creative process is inherently personal and subjective, a reflection of your unique perspective and experiences. It is a courageous act to bring forth something new into the world, something that did not exist before you imagined it into being. This act alone is worthy of recognition, irrespective of its reception. To maintain confidence and self-worth, one must cultivate a resilient inner dialogue. Speak to yourself with kindness and compassion, as you would to a dear friend. Remind yourself of your achievements, your growth, and the times you have overcome adversity. This internal narrative is a sanctuary, a place where the words of others cannot reach unless you permit them entry. Strategic repetition of affirmations can fortify this sanctuary. A mantra such as "I can achieve, my creativity is valid, and my effort has value" can serve as a bulwark against the waves of doubt that criticism may bring. Repeat it, believe in it, let it resonate within you until it becomes an integral part of your creative ethos.

It is also crucial to differentiate between constructive criticism and destructive commentary. Constructive criticism, offered with respect and aimed at helping you grow, can be a valuable tool. It provides an opportunity for reflection and learning. On the other hand, destructive commentary, which is often rooted in the critic's own insecurities or malice, should be acknowledged for what it is—a reflection of the critic, not of your work or your worth. Maintaining confidence and self-worth requires the strategic cultivation of perspective. When faced with criticism, step back and consider the broader view. Ask yourself: Will this matter in five years? Is this an opportunity to learn something new about my craft? By adopting a growth-oriented mindset, you can transform criticism from a source of pain into a catalyst for development.

Transformative Perspectives on Constructive Feedback

The Gift of Growth: Embracing Opportunities for Improvement — Constructive feedback should be seen as a gift rather than a personal attack. It provides valuable insights into areas where we can grow and improve. When someone takes the time to offer feedback, it is a sign that they believe in our potential and want to see us succeed. By reframing feedback as an opportunity for growth, we can approach it with an open mind and a willingness to learn.

The Power of Perspective: Gaining New Insights — Constructive feedback offers a fresh perspective on our work. It allows us to see our creations through the eyes of others and gain insights that we may have overlooked. By embracing different viewpoints, we expand our creative horizons and challenge our preconceived notions. This shift in perspective can lead to innovative breakthroughs and push us to explore new creative possibilities.

Separating the Art from the Artist: Detaching Self-Worth from Feedback — It is crucial to separate our self-worth from the feedback we receive. Constructive criticism is not a reflection of our value as individuals but rather an evaluation of our work within a specific context. By detaching ourselves from the feedback, we can approach it with objectivity and use it as a tool for improvement. Remember, the feedback is about the work, not about you as a person.

Feedback as a Dialogue: Fostering Collaboration and Connection — Constructive feedback is not a one-way street. It is an invitation to engage in a dialogue with others who share a passion for our work. By viewing feedback as a collaborative process, we can create meaningful connections and build a supportive creative community. Embrace the opportunity to ask questions, seek clarification, and exchange ideas. Through open communication, we can deepen our understanding of our work and forge valuable relationships.

The Evolution of Art: Embracing Change and Growth — Art is not static; it is an ever-evolving expression of our creative journey. Constructive feedback reminds us that our work is not set in stone but is meant to evolve and grow. Embrace feedback as a catalyst for change and allow it to push you outside your comfort zone. Embracing the transformative power of feedback opens up new possibilities for artistic exploration and personal development.

Chapter 8: Embracing Failure and Growth

Failure as a Natural Part of the Creative Process

Contextualising failure begins with a nuanced redefinition. Failure, in the eyes of a therapist, is not a dead end but rather a divergent path—one that invites exploration, not retreat. It is a construct, often laden with the weight of societal stigma, yet devoid of inherent meaning until we choose to interpret its essence. Through the therapeutic lens, we learn that failure is not the opposite of success; it is an integral phase in the continuum towards success.

Consider the great masters of art, literature, and music; their legacies are not solely composed of relentless triumphs but are punctuated by a series of missteps, rejections, and blunders. Beethoven's symphonies were not birthed without discordant notes. Picasso's masterpieces did not emerge without errant lines. Their greatness was not defined by an absence of failure but by their resilience in its presence. If we assimilate the therapeutic perspective that every failed attempt is rich with potential for self-discovery and skill refinement. When a novel remains unpublished, a painting unsold, or a melody unheard, it is not an indictment of worth but an invitation to introspection. What can be gleaned from this experience? Which aspects of our work resonated, and which fell flat? A therapist would guide us to extract the lessons nestled within the heart of failure and to wield them as tools for our next venture.

The therapeutic process teaches us to strip failure of its power to induce shame. Instead, it becomes a catalyst for a dialogue with our inner selves about our values, goals, and strategies. It prompts us to question, to challenge, to grow. In therapy, we learn to sit with discomfort, to hold it gently, to understand its contours and textures. We adopt a stance of curiosity rather than criticism, allowing us to reframe setbacks as stepping stones on the path to mastery. The entrepreneur's journey is inherently creative, one that stares into uncertainty. Here, failure is not a misstep but part of the journey. It is within this intricate interplay that our creative spirit is tested and tempered.

Embrace our humanity. We acknowledge that failure is universally woven into the human experience, and in doing so, we connect with the broader tapestry of those who create and endeavor. The shared experience of overcoming adversity can be a unifying thread in the fabric of our collective artistic endeavor.

Strategies for Reframing Failure as a Catalyst for Success

Here, we explore five transformative techniques that can serve as alchemical tools, transmuting the leaden weight of failure into the golden light of success.

Mindful Acknowledgement — Before you can begin to reframe failure, you must first acknowledge its presence without judgment or self-reproach. This is a moment of mindful acceptance, a therapeutic embrace that says, "Yes, I have failed, and that's acceptable." Taking a leaf from mindfulness practices, observe your failure as if from a distance – note its contours, its texture, its impact. A failure acknowledged is divested of its stealthy power, its ability to sabotage your continuing endeavors from the shadows.

Analytical Deconstruction — With acknowledgment comes the power to dissect. Engage in a post-mortem analysis, but not with the cold detachment of a coroner. Rather, think of yourself as an archaeologist uncovering the precious artifacts of wisdom buried beneath the rubble of your failed attempts. Deconstruct the elements: What worked? What did not? Where did the pivots turn too sharply? By mapping the anatomy of your failure, you prepare the groundwork for building more resilient strategies.

Positive Reframing — The art of positive reframing is not about donning rose-colored spectacles to view your past failures. Instead, it is a creative endeavor, much like applying a new coat of varnish to a cherished piece of furniture. It reveals the beauty underneath the wear and tear. Identify and emphasize any silver linings – maybe a venture did not succeed as planned, but perhaps it led you to valuable connections or taught you skills that will serve you in future projects.

Strategic Integration — Now comes the stage where we move from contemplation to action. Strategic integration involves taking the insights gleaned from your past failures and folding them into your future plans. It is a melding of theory and experience, with each setback providing concrete steps for improvement. Consider tactical adjustments such as developing new competencies or tweaking your business model. These strategies are the phoenix feathers, emblematic of rebirth from ashes.

Passionate Perseverance — Finally, leverage your passion to fuel your perseverance. Failure often leads to an introspective quest, pushing us to question our purpose and resolve. By reconnecting with the passion that set you on this path initially, you can find the strength to persist. Passionate perseverance is about channeling your deepest motivations into a tenacious pursuit of your goals, recognising that each failure brings you one step closer to success.

Integrate some of these techniques into your daily praxis. Just as the masterful sculptor does not despise the chisel for an errant stroke but wields it with greater skill on the next endeavor, so must you embrace failure as an indispensable tool in your artistic arsenal. Through these strategies of reframing failure, you will learn that it is not the antithesis of success but rather an intrinsic element of it. Each misstep is a lesson, every setback a course correction – and when failure ceases to be feared, it can be employed as a powerful catalyst for personal and professional growth.

Failures and Strategic Shifts in Art History

The creative landscape is filled with tales of those who, having encountered the rugged terrain of failure, managed not only to survive but to succeed. Every misshapen clay of misfortune contributed to their legacies. Let us bear witness to the transformative power of failure and pivot.

Consider the illustrious life of Vincent van Gogh, an artist whose name resonates with brilliance, yet whose existence was marred by despair and rejection. Today, his artworks are treasures, gracing the walls of the most esteemed galleries. But in his time? Van Gogh was a man plagued by anxiety, a soul seldom at peace with himself or his milieu. He sold but a single painting in his lifetime. Imagine, then, the fortitude required to persist in his creative pursuit despite such pervasive disconfirmation. Van Gogh's story is one of profound resilience; his posthumous fame, a poignant reminder that the merit of one's art may only find its recognition beyond the periphery of one's own epoch.

Transitioning forward in time, we encounter the jazz titan Billie Holiday. An artist whose voice could cradle the most turbulent emotions, she faced adversity both personal and professional. Her battles with addiction and her skirmishes with a society that seldom treated her with the dignity she deserved are well-documented. Yet through this cacophony of challenges, Holiday's artistry soared. Her ability to embed her struggles into the soul-stirring timbre of her music speaks to the heart's capacity to transfigure pain into unmatched beauty.

Another profound case is that of J.K. Rowling, a contemporary beacon of literary success whose early career was fraught with rejection and financial strife. The manuscript of 'Harry Potter' faced numerous rejections before finding its home with a publisher willing to take a chance on a story about a boy wizard. Rowling's unrelenting belief in her narrative, coupled with an unwavering dedication to her craft, ultimately engendered a cultural phenomenon that redefined children's literature and captivated readers across generations.

These stories illustrate the relationship between failure and growth. The narrative arc of these artists does not follow the linear path of instant triumph but rather winds through the valleys of despair and ascends the peaks of eventual recognition. What lessons may we glean from their journeys? One that pivotal moments arise not only from external validation but from an internal wellspring of faith—a belief in one's own vision that defies the transient opinions of critics and naysayers.

These narratives teach us that a pivot does not signify a wholesale abandonment of one's essence. It is the strategic reorientation of one's compass when the original path leads to a dead-end—an adjustment in course that retains the core while responding with agility to the ever-shifting landscape of life and art.

Chapter 9: Nurturing Creativity and Inspiration in Everyday Life

Embracing a growth mindset and continuous learning

Just like a vast and dynamic ocean, our voyage is graced by brilliant sunrises and occasionally threatened by violent storms. One of the most potent gales we can harness is a growth mindset, an approach to life that embraces learning as a cherished companion on our journey. With roots in psychological theory, the concept of a growth mindset was first introduced by psychologist Carol Dweck as an antidote to the 'fixed mindset', which believes abilities are set in stone and largely unaffected by effort.

In contrast, a growth mindset sees failures not as indications of incompetence but as signposts towards success, directing us to areas that require further learning. It does not attribute setbacks to immutable qualities, like talent or intelligence, but appreciates them as part of a voyage that is inevitably marked by moments of stormy weather. We ride on the waves of novelty; our work thrives on our ability to see fresh perspectives, to construct original concepts, to innovate, iterate, and inspire. Each day presents an opportunity for growth, for learning something new, for creating a better version of our artistry. But growth is not an auto-pilot function; it requires conscious effort, deliberate practice, and thoughtful reflection. It requires us to unlearn notions of 'perfection' and adopt the humbling attitude of a perpetual student.

The growth mindset extends beyond the confines of our creative endeavors—it influences our relationship with ourselves, with others, and with the world. It underpins our potential to evolve, innovate, and adapt, especially when navigating the often turbulent waters of entrepreneurship. Stoking the fires of a growth mindset in our everyday lives means not merely surviving these waters but transforming them into a source of strength, of inspiration, of authentic creativity. Cultivating a growth mindset is akin to growing a garden; it requires daily dedication, nurturing, and gentle patience. Let your experiences be your sunlight, the nourishment that allows you to flourish.

Fostering Creativity through Environment and Workspace Design

To achieve the much-coveted state of getting lost in the creative flow, it necessitates more than just willpower. Our environment—our creative warren, if you will—exerts a profound influence on our mental states and capabilities. Infused with entrepreneurial wisdom and psychological insights, let's explore the role of environment in shaping our creative self.

Drifting back to my earlier days as an entrepreneur, ensnared in the lashings of my own anxieties, what strikes me most strongly was the impact of my physical workspace. My desk was often a cacophony of clutter. Stacks of papers piled high, half-empty cups of coffee teetering dangerously, pens strewn like fallen soldiers. The message it broadcast to my brain? Chaos. A disordered space is a disordered mind, and my creative energy drowned in this tumult. The psychological concept of neuro-architecture teaches us that our environment influences our cognition and behavior. A cluttered workspace can lead to a mind shackled in cognitive clutter, inhibiting the free flow of ideas. The question then arises - how do we architect our environment to foster our creative prowess?

Understand that creativity isn't merely a cognitive process; it's an emotional one too. Our environment should be an external reflection of our internal state. We must align the space around us with the emotions conducive to creativity - tranquility, joy, curiosity. This may manifest as a picture of that hiking expedition that left you awestruck or an artifact that stokes the fires of your intellectual curiosity.

Next, eliminate distractions. In an era of buzzes and dings, our attention is a fortress under constant siege. Organize your workspace in such a way that it bolsters your defenses against these marauders of mental calm. Perhaps this means using noise-canceling headphones or setting specific times for perusing emails. More practical considerations involve the strategic use of light and color. Ample natural light has been associated with improved mood, alertness, and even meta-cognition—our awareness of our own cognitive processes. Color, too, can influence our psychological states. Blue and green hues, for example, have been found to stimulate creativity, perhaps by subconsciously reminding us of the natural world, a veritable playground of novelty. Incorporate elements of nature into your workspace. Biophilic design—an approach that seeks to connect people more closely to nature—can enhance clarity of thought, and improve wellbeing. This may involve having houseplants at your workspace or working in environments with a view of green spaces.

Remember though, no two creative minds mirror each other precisely. Some flourish in silence; others burst with creativity amidst a symphony of sounds. Some need a sanctuary of solitude; others thrive on the vibrancy of interactions. The key is mindful observation – of observing your working styles, your response to different stimulations, and crafting your environment accordingly. There's great power in shaping our environment in ways that nurture our creative spirit. It's like creating a bed of fertile soil where the seeds of our ideas can take root and blossom. As we apply this therapeutic wisdom to our creative entrepreneurial journey, we aren't just organizing spaces; we are curating ecosystems for our ideas to thrive. As you look around your workspace, think not just of what it is, but of what it could be—a nerve center for your innovation, a sanctuary for your creativity. It's more than physical space. It's mental space. A realm where you and your creativity can truly dance in harmony. So, create meticulously, my fellow innovators. For creativity isn't merely a state of mind; it's also a state of place.

The Art of Balancing Rest and Productivity for Creative Success

A sigh of relief often accompanies the closing of our laptops, signifying the act of officially 'clocking out' from the rigorous entrepreneurial pursuits. However, as creative entrepreneurs, we must maintain a delicate equilibrium between the worlds of productivity and rest, both integral to fostering a climate ripe for creativity. The yielding of fruitful creative outcomes is not solely a product of relentless hustling. It also intimately hinges on the incorporation of rest, allowing our minds to refresh and our beings to reconnect with the essence of our creative core. Rest, in this context, is not the indolent act of idleness, but a deliberate and purposeful disengagement from the immediate demands of creative entrepreneurship. Aristotle once mused, "Whosoever is delighted in solitude is either a wild beast or a god." Within this solitude, within this rest, lies the gestation period for our most transcendent creative ideas. This solitude is the birthplace of authenticity—the very hallmark of a thriving creative entrepreneur.

Embrace rest like an old friend. Welcome it with open arms, not as an unwelcome intruder disrupting your momentum, but as a necessary ally in your creative voyage. These are the moments when abstract thoughts solidify into groundbreaking ideas, when inadequate notions evolve into whole-hearted concepts, and when mere inklings mature into life-altering beliefs that propel you forward on your journey. To begin this journey of inviting rest into our lives, we must first understand and acknowledge the prevalent 'hustle culture' circulating the entrepreneurial ecosystem. This culture often glorifies relentless work while belittling the necessity for rest. It grooms us into equating our worth with our productivity, a harmful paradigm requiring immediate dismantling.

As you begin to tiptoe out of this hustle culture, perceive it not as wasting time. Instead, view this time as an investment in your mental health and wellbeing. This shift—a shift from seeing time spent resting as wasted, to perceiving it as invested—marks the first significant stride towards nurturing creativity. We need to actively unlearn the negative connotations attached to rest and realize the immense potential it harbours. Just as a harpist cannot play a harmonious melody without the silence between the notes, an artist cannot create without periods of rest between vigorous bouts of work. Perhaps integrating small, restful habits into your daily routine could be your starting point. It could be as simple as a five-minute meditation practice amid a hectic workday or a leisurely walk in nature to cleanse your creative palate.

In the midst of this rest, empower your mind to wander, to contemplate, to dream. Allow it to delve into the realms of the impossible, exploring uncharted territories, and fostering an insatiable curiosity—a cornerstone of all creative pursuits. Remember, embracing a balance between rest and productivity is not a compromise but a commitment—a commitment to your wellbeing, your creativity, and ultimately, your authenticity. This growth-oriented rhythm is integral to fostering a thriving creative entrepreneur within you.

Exercises for a Growth Mindset

Creative entrepreneurs inherently grope with risky challenges, stepping off the beaten path and courageously embracing the unknown. In doing so, they often face anxiety and self-doubt. However, utilizing therapeutic exercises can help them cultivate a growth mindset essential for creative flourishing. Let's delve into four such therapeutic techniques.

The Magic of Mindful Reflection — Mindful reflection is an act of exploring the self, cultivating consciousness of our thoughts, feelings, and experiences. For a creative entrepreneur, this exercise can be an introspective journey where they cherish every step of their creative process, detached from the anxieties of the future or regrets of the past. Mindful reflection allows creative entrepreneurs to know their thoughts and feelings better, aiding them to handle their anxiety more healthily. This method helps build a greater sense of self-awareness and promotes a growth-oriented attitude.

Visualization: The Creative Catalyst — Visualization is an artistic exercise that can catalyze creativity, empowering us to see beyond the obvious, think unconventionally, and take bold steps towards the unknown. By visualizing their creative success, entrepreneurs can align their subconscious mind with their conscious efforts. This alignment helps reduce anxiety and foster a growth mindset, thus unlocking the doors to creative innovation and exploration.

Journaling: The Therapeutic Pathway To Self-Understanding — Journaling, in essence, is a personal narrative, a tale of our thoughts and feelings. It helps distill our mental wanderings into coherent reflections, opening a therapeutic pathway to self-understanding. For a creative entrepreneur, journaling can be a canvas where they articulate their anxieties, fears, ambitions, and dreams. This contemplative exercise helps map the mind's landscape, enabling them to recognize their anxiety triggers, celebrate their wins, and plan their creative path more mindfully.

The Roots of Resilience — It is within the rich soil of past experiences that we plant the seeds for future resilience. Start this exercise by recounting instances where you overcame adversity. Reflect deeply in your journal, not only on the outcomes but also on the inner resources you cultivated. Like roots digging deeper in search of sustenance, let these reflections draw strength from the fertile ground of your history. Such introspection is a therapeutic reminder that even in moments of strife, you are nurturing a resilient core.

"What If?" — Venture into the mental garden of "What If?" and sow seeds of courageous thoughts. Ask yourself, what if I viewed this creative block as an invitation to innovate? What if this criticism is the secret key to my next artistic breakthrough? Allow these seeds to take root, watered by the belief that each setback is a herald of growth. As these thoughts blossom into a garden of possibilities, you'll find your creative journey enriched with a greater sense of purpose and invigoration.

The Symphony of Small Wins — In the grand symphony of achieving our artistic visions, it is the notes of small wins that create an encouraging melody. This exercise involves setting micro-goals, tiny but achievable objectives that lead toward your larger ambition. Ticking off these goals is akin to playing scales on a piano — each small success is a note that contributes to your overall mastery. Acknowledge each small victory with a celebratory pause, like the rests in music that give depth and rhythm to a piece. Through these therapeutic exercises, you build not only skills but also trust in your ability to progress, measure by measure.

These therapeutic exercises are not just disparate techniques, but they merge to form a holistic approach to build a growth mindset, with each exercise complementing the other in a symphony of self-growth. Mindful reflection sets the stage for self-awareness, positive affirmations reshape our belief system, visualization aligns our subconscious and conscious efforts, and journaling provides a reflective platform capturing our inner journey. Thus, these techniques weave together to foster resilience, encourage growth, and help creative entrepreneurs rise above their anxieties and reach the pinnacle of their creative expression.

Let us remember: anxiety and self-doubt may occasionally shadow the path of creativity, yet they can be surmounted. With these therapeutic exercises, creative entrepreneurs can transform their mindset from mere surviving to thriving, stoking their inner fire of creativity towards the art of authentic entrepreneurial brilliance.

Chapter 10: Authenticity in Creative Entrepreneurship

Understanding Authenticity

Authenticity is the characteristic that distinguishes us from the rest, an attribute that we desperately need within our respective crafts. But what is authenticity, really? How can we define something that seems so nebulous, so subjective? Does it lie within our personal values? Our creative process? Or perhaps it's hidden within the intersection of both? When we speak of authenticity, we're referring to the quality of being genuine, real, and true to oneself. It is retaining our distinctiveness in a world that seems to continually blur individuality. Authenticity is the courage to share our unique perspectives, novel ideas borne from original thought and painted with the vibrant colors of experience. It refers to the ability to remain faithful to oneself, exhibit sincerity in our words and actions, and align them with our deepest beliefs and values.

In the vast, pioneering world of creative entrepreneurship, authenticity is the spark that sets us apart. It is in our unique creative expressions, in our refusal to merely imitate or blend into the homogeneous background. It's the audacious statement that boldly says, "I am here, and this is my work." It is crucial to appreciate, though, that authenticity is not static - it is fluid, evolving just as we do. It's not a single checkpoint we arrive, but wherein we continuously refine our understanding of ourselves and our craft. Authenticity is dynamic;

It can be challenging to harness authenticity, given the external pressures and societal expectations that surround us. The fear of exposure, of revealing ourselves and our creative processes, can be daunting. We may be assailed by doubts, questioning if our creations are 'good enough,' 'interesting enough,' or 'different enough.' When confronted with such anxiety, we must remind ourselves that our authenticity is not defined by others' perceptions but by our alignment with our deeper selves.

Let's reflect: What draws us to our craft? What enthralls us? What are the core values that guide our decisions? By answering these fundamental questions, we can excavate the bedrock of our authenticity which we can then infuse into our work. Authenticity is an invisible signature etched into our creations. It's a personal statement that says, "This is who I am, this is my perspective, and this is how I see the world." It doesn't strive for universal acceptance or appreciation, it instead seeks to connect with those who resonate with its unique energy. Authenticity is a journey inward, a transformative archaeological exploration, where we unearth our deepest values, passions, and strengths. Once discovered, these qualities merge into our work where they shine brightly for all to see.

The Relationship between Authenticity and Anxiety

Authenticity, that genuine alignment between one's internal life and external expression, holds a pivotal role in the creative journey. Consider authenticity as it keeps us rooted in who we genuinely are, providing a compass-point amid the tumultuous world of entrepreneurship. It invites us to remember, even as the tides of trends and opinion surge around us, the substance of who we are, our values, our visions, and our voice. It whispers to us that our worth is not tethered to external validation but to the depth of our integrity and the resonance of our truth.

But what arises when this authentic selfhood seems threatened? When a tsunami of change, criticism, or commercial pressures jeopardizes our core sense of self? The result is often anxiety—marked by apprehension, excessive worry, and restlessness, chiefly fueled by a sense of impending threat. It's the psyche's alarm system, signaling a perceived danger to our wellbeing. In this context, that danger is the disconnection from our authentic selves. Ergo, when we feel compelled to compromise our authenticity—to reshuffle our values to fit a mold, to dilute our voice to please the masses, to lose ourselves amid the demands and expectations of entrepreneurship—our internal alarm bells begin to ring. It's a mental tug-of-war between the urge to conform and the desire to remain true to ourselves. This incongruity breeds anxiety.

Psychology beckons us to view anxiety not merely as an adversary but also as an ally. Carl Jung, the trailblazer of analytical psychology, suggested that the 'tension of opposites' can lead to a higher third, a transcendental function— a state of mind that transcends the conflict, thus engendering growth. Herein lies our philosophical reflection. If anxiety is the tension arising from perceived threats to our authenticity, could we not convert this tension into a driving force propelling us towards greater genuineness? An anxiety that does not paralyze, but energizes; an anxiety that does not constrict, but liberates; an anxiety that navigates us through uncharted waters into a harbour of self-understanding and self-acceptance.

Soren Kierkegaard, the father of existentialism, profoundly stated, "Anxiety is the dizziness of freedom." And it is in this space of 'dizziness,' between the world's expectations and our internal truths, where we encounter our freedom—our freedom to choose authenticity, to esteem truth over trend, substance over spectacle.

Authentic Leadership

Authentic leadership is the cornerstone of successful creative entrepreneurship. It asks us to look within ourselves, to distill our essence into how we lead, manage, and create. It calls upon us to defying societal expectations and norms, to draw strength from our core values and express them in meaningful, transformative ways. In a world that often encourages us to fashion ourselves in certain molds, authentic leadership is a rebellion. It is an opting-out of predefined pathways and an intentional journey towards the uncharted territories of our individuality.

Before we delve further into this existential territory, let's pause for a brief moment. Reflect on these questions: Are you gratified with the leadership you currently exhibit in your creative enterprise? Are you leading from a place of authenticity, or do you often feel you're pretending, playing a part that doesn't align with your true essence? In the realm of creative entrepreneurship, the opportunity to lead authentically is omnipresent. The decisions we make; the way we manage time, resources and people; the creations we bring forth; all represent avenues to extend our authentic selves into the world around us. To embody authentic leadership, the first task is to identify your core values. What motivates you? What do you believe in? What is your vision for your creative enterprise, and how do you wish to lead your team, or indeed yourself, towards it? Understanding your values points towards authenticity. It encourages us to reject external influences that could sway us off our course and prompts us to stay grounded in our truth.

The next task is to cultivate transparency. Authenticity is intrinsically tied to openness—being open about our strengths, weaknesses, success, failures, aspirations, and fears. Transparency is unsettling at times, mainly due to the vulnerability it demands. But remember, there is power in vulnerability. The capacity to be vulnerable by expressing our authentic selves in our leadership and creativity is empowering.

The journey towards authentic leadership is ultimately a journey home—to our core, the essence of who we are. It is a voyage worth undertaking for the sake of our creativity, our enterprise, and indeed, ourselves.

Steps to Becoming More Authentic

Authenticity is not about mimicry or imitation, rather it's about embracing originality and distinctiveness. It involves breaking free from societal molds, definitions of success, and creative norms. It is a courageous act of self-assertion and a genuine portrayal of self, creativity, and entrepreneurship. This process of becoming authentic requires introspection, awareness, courage, and patience.

Step 1: Embrace Self-Awareness – The journey towards authenticity starts with self-awareness. It's about viewing yourself through an unbiased lens, acknowledging both your strengths and weaknesses. It involves introspection and reflective contemplation. You must ask, "What drives me?" "What are my core values?" "What brings me joy and fulfillment?" The answers to these questions create a blueprint of your authentic self.

Step 2: Acknowledge Your Unique Creative Vision – Every creative entrepreneur possesses a unique vision. This vision is often a reflection of their personal experiences, influences, aspirations, and values. Acknowledging your unique creative vision is an essential step towards authenticity. Articulate this vision honestly and assertively in your creative expressions and entrepreneurial ventures.

Step 3: Courageously Confront Fear and Doubt – Becoming more authentic means confronting fear and self-doubt – those stifling forces that inhibit us from expressing our true selves. Therapy might throw light on why we construct protective layers. It's crucial to remember that fear and doubt are part of the human journey. Recognizing them enables us to replace self-critical thoughts with more compassionate narratives.

Step 4: Align Actions and Decisions with Core Values – Authenticity is reflected in every decision and action we take. Therefore, it's essential to align these with our core values. An artist whose core value is authenticity, might refuse projects that demand them to compromise their artistic integrity. An entrepreneur guided by innovation would not resort to conventional business practices that stifle creativity.

Step 5: Practice Openness and Honesty – Being authentic means being honest and open, not just with others, but primarily with oneself. This honesty allows us to accept our flaws and celebrate our strengths. It gives us the courage to try, fail, learn, and evolve, thereby fostering growth both as an individual and an artist.

Step 6: Cultivate Consistency – Authenticity is not a one-time achievement, but a continuous journey. Therefore, it's crucial to maintain consistency in honoring your true self. Consistency creates trust, enables meaningful connections, and improves credibility in your entrepreneurial journey.

Building an Authentic Brand

The crafting of our brand is a reflection of our journey, a testament to our passion, creativity, and a mirror of our authenticity. It is not merely a logo, a catchy tagline, or a slick website. No, it is the distillation of our beliefs, values, experiences, and talents.

To establish an authentic brand, we embark on a journey of self-knowledge, of understanding our values, motivations, and unique strengths from a place of depth and honesty. So, how do you forge an authentic brand? This path should not intimidate you; instead, view it as an artistic adventure, just as you approach every creative endeavor.

First and foremost, understand your 'why'. The 'why' is the emotional root, the driving force behind what you do. It serves as the compass for your entrepreneurial journey and should resonate profoundly in your brand. Reflect on this: Why do you create what you create? Why should others care about your creations? Why do you get up every morning eager to create? Your 'why' encapsulates your passion, your purpose, and ultimately, your authenticity. It should genuinely resonate with you and radiate through every aspect of your brand.

Next, mold your 'how' and 'what'. The 'how' signifies your unique approach to your craft, your distinct technique, and your philosophy. It characterizes how you bring your 'why' to life. The 'what', on the other hand, is the manifestation of your craft – your products or services. Both the 'how' and 'what' must align with your 'why', thereby forming a cohesive, authentic brand identity.

Also, bear in mind that authenticity does not equate to perfection. Quite the contrary. It involves embracing your quirks, your peculiarities, and even your flaws. It means owning your story with courage, vulnerability, and integrity. **Remember, a polished, glossy facade might initially attract attention, but it's authenticity that breeds trust and fosters loyalty.** Authenticity has a peculiar enchantment; it draws people closer. A brand that is authentic becomes more than a business; it cultivates a community of like-minded individuals who resonate with its values and story.

Dare to bring your authentic self into every facet of your brand. Use it as your north star while navigating the enduring dance between creativity and entrepreneurship. In doing so, you'll not only construct a brand that is genuine and compelling, but you'll also build a legacy that stands the test of time. Be patient with yourself and your brand. Cultivate it with time, and give it the space to breathe, grow, and transform along with you. Authenticity is more potent than any marketing strategy. It is the lifeblood that pulses through every successful venture. It is, indeed, an immeasurable form of artistic expression in itself. It is your key to a thriving creative business.

Authenticity and Business Success

Authenticity has emerged as a critical component within the contemporary creative landscape that cannot be overlooked. You can find myriad successful creative entrepreneurs who have been able to construct impressive business empires on the bedrock of authentic expression. What, then, is the link between authenticity and business success? The answer lies in the unique value that authenticity brings to the proverbial table – a value that is increasingly sought after in contemporary society, characterized by an emphasis on individualism, self-expression, and innovation.

Authenticity allows entrepreneurs to create a distinctive, recognizable brand that reflects their true self. This genuineness breeds trust and loyalty among customers, who appreciate authenticity in a world saturated with manipulation and pretense. When you consistently present yourself with honesty and integrity, you effectively distinguish yourself in the crowded entrepreneurial landscape, making your creative outputs uniquely attractive. The philosophical axiom of 'being true to oneself' extends beyond personal development to entrepreneurial success. Operating authentically provides a foundation for consistent decision-making and a clear vision, eliminating the psychological friction that comes with contradiction. This aligns your creative energies towards a single purpose, maximizes productivity, and provides a clearer path towards your goals. We find that it is authenticity's unique appeal that sets an enterprise apart. In a world cluttered with generic repetition, consumers are increasingly drawn towards authenticity. Thus, when entrepreneurs consistently showcase their true selves, they build a distinctive personal brand that resonates with the audience and cultivates their trust and loyalty.

The life of Ai Weiwei proves testament to this idea. A renowned artist and activist, Weiwei stands as a compelling testament to the inseparable fusion of personal experiences and political convictions within an artist's work. Born in Beijing in 1957, he grew up during a period of immense political and social upheaval in China. His father, the renowned poet Ai Qing, fell victim to political persecution, and this familial turbulence undoubtedly left an indelible mark on Weiwei's worldview. Through his body of work, he has demonstrated a persistent, unapologetic commitment to shining a light on social injustices and state corruption, even in the face of severe government surveillance. Notably, his 2011 detention by Chinese authorities for his outspoken activism only strengthened his resolve, turning him into a symbol of resistance against authoritarianism. Ai Weiwei's unyielding dedication to his craft and his fearless pursuit of truth through art underscore the transformative power of creativity in the face of adversity.

Despite being monitored, arrested, and silenced numerous times, Ai Weiwei has remained unwaveringly authentic to his purpose and vision, crafting art that is as true to himself as it is provocative to his audience and critics. This authentic approach to his artistry is, in large measure, responsible for garnering Ai Weiwei international acclaim. He has succeeded in making a global impact not just because of his technical virtuosity and innovative use of materials but also because he infuses every artwork with his own lived experiences and critical social perspectives. Viewers from all around the world are drawn to his work because it resonates on a profoundly human level, transcending cultural boundaries and political divides.

Similarly, Banksy, whose identity remains a closely guarded secret, uses art is primarily showcased on the streets, catching the attention of passersby with its stark commentary on sociopolitical issues. His preferred canvas, the urban landscape, allows him to speak directly to the masses. Despite the cloak of anonymity, there is an undeniable authenticity in his art. From his distinctive technique to his powerful imagery and satirical epigrams, Banksy continues to create works that are unapologetically true to his artistic vision. His frequent themes of anti-war, anti-capitalism, and anti-establishment reveal a deep reflection of current affairs and society's misgivings.

Banksy's authenticity does more than just demonstrate his artistic prowess; it resonates with people around the globe. His ability to convey complex, controversial themes through simple, amusing, yet poignant pieces has led to a zealous following. By transforming walls, bridges, and streets into his exhibition spaces, he invites everyone, regardless of societal status or artistic inclination, to interpret and appreciate his work. People feel a connection to his art, regardless of cultural, political, or geographical barriers, because of its widely relatable themes and its reflection of shared human experiences and emotions. His work now commands millions at auctions, transforming, what was once considered a public nuisance, into a respected and valued art form. Collectors and art enthusiasts alike see the value in his work, and the demand for original Banksy pieces continues to grow. Thus, Banksy's authenticity as an artist has not only revolutionized street art, but it has also made him a successful creative entrepreneur.

From a business perspective, authenticity attracts a loyal audience and opens the door for collaborations with like-minded individuals who align with your values. It germinates an entrepreneurial ecosystem where integrity and individuality bloom alongside creativity and innovation. However, authenticity is not a magic potion that guarantees instant success. It's about making risky decisions that align with your convictions, continually reflecting on motives and actions, and persevering when faced with adversity. Embracing authenticity is not always an easy task, particularly in a competitive business world that often incentivizes conformity. It demands courage, self-awareness, and resilience. Courage, to stand firm in your values in the face of criticism or resistance. Self-awareness, to continually reflect on your values, motives, and actions. And resilience, to maintain your commitment to authenticity when facing challenges.

The more you align your entrepreneurial journey with your genuine self, the more you will find your work fulfilling. This fulfillment not just fuels your creative spirit, but also ignites the passion required to overcome the inevitable challenges that arise on the path to success. An authentic brand not only attracts loyal customers but also like-minded collaborators who can contribute to your entrepreneurial journey. Thus, from both a business and psychological perspective, authenticity stands at the heart of entrepreneurial success. You are empowered to create and contribute in ways that are truly unique and impactful.

Chapter 11: Enhancing Productivity and Creativity

Time Management for Creative Entrepreneurs

Success, both within the realm of creativity and beyond, invariably requires the crossing of a metaphorical wasteland: a terrain where time is the most precious commodity and managing it, an art form unto itself. The creative entrepreneur, the weaver of ideas and architect of dreams, knows this better than anyone. Their minds, constantly teeming with an inexhaustible rush of inventive, ground-breaking ideas, are also perpetually faced with the formidable challenge of harnessing the tumultuous flow and directing it profitably. To successfully navigate the terrain of creativity and entrepreneurship, one must learn to master the dextrous art of time management. It is not, as one may initially presume, a rigid set of rules that stifles creativity, but can, in fact, serve as its scaffold, providing our ideas with structure and direction.

The first step towards achieving this equilibrium between creativity and productivity is by embracing a mindful approach to time. One must first acknowledge that time is finite. This simple realization serves as a powerful catalyst for maximizing our day, propelling us to prioritize tasks, eliminate distractions and focus our energies on what truly matters - our creative endeavors.

The concept of "Time Blocking" is an effective method that wrangles time into manageable segments. An approach much like the act of painting a canvas – block by block, color by color until a masterpiece is formed. You entire day, week, or even month, becomes that canvas. Each task, be it brainstorming for a new project, sketching a design, responding to emails, or maintaining your social media presence, becomes a color or shade. You paint your week with these tasks, assigning each a specific block of time. This way, each task gets its moment in the spotlight and more importantly, other tasks do not encroach on this dedicated time. Imagine a composer, sitting down at his grand piano, staring at a blank score. He doesn't just hack away at the keys in a haphazard fashion, but carefully plans and structures each note, each chord, each measure, to create a symphony. That is what time blocking is - it's composing your day, your week, your life in such a way that every moment is a note in the symphony of your productivity.

For those who find their creativity isn't consistently predictable, not willing to be tamed into preordained time blocks, "The Flow Technique" could be the answer. As an artist, your most profound ideas and breakthrough moments might not arrive at a predetermined hour. Hence, the Flow Technique encourages spontaneity. When the flurry of creativity descends, you allow yourself to ride the wave entirely, disregarding any planned tasks. However, ensuring productivity and avoiding procrastination, it is essential to also designate 'Catch-up Blocks' in your week where postponed tasks are attended to.

The "1-3-5 Rule" is another method to infuse your day with a sense of structured flexibility. Under this rule, you set one large goal, three medium tasks, and five small tasks to accomplish over the day. The flexibility here lies in the definition of small, medium, and large tasks. As a creative mind, your 'large' goal could be as tangible as finishing a piece or as intangible as finding the inspiration for your next project. Let's explore this considering the story of Samantha. Her initial approach to work was chaotic, attempting to handle everything and anything that came her way. However, the "1-3-5 rule" provided categorizing her tasks based on their scale and importance. She focused her cognitive resources on one significant task, like securing a new client or developing a new product. Then, she managed three medium tasks, perhaps meetings or team briefings, and then five smaller tasks like responding to emails or updating social media.

Another effective strategy is the "Eisenhower Box", based on a quote attributed to Dwight D. Eisenhower: "I have two kinds of problems, the urgent and the important. The urgent are not important, and the important are never urgent." This method categorizes tasks into four categories: urgent and important; important, but not urgent; urgent but not important; and not important or urgent. The Eisenhower Box efficiently balances immediate needs with long-term goals, a key skill for a successful creative entrepreneur. In the process of implementing the Eisenhower Box, one becomes a mindful entrepreneur. It is not a mere scheduling technique, but rather an exercise in introspection and strategic thinking. Every task is examined under the microscope of urgency and importance, a practice that requires self-awareness and objectivity. For instance, a business meeting may seem urgent, but if it does not directly contribute to your long-term goals, it may fall under the Not Important but Urgent quadrant. Meanwhile, reading a book to enhance your knowledge may not seem urgent but is important for your personal growth and therefore belongs to the Important but Not Urgent quadrant. The Eisenhower Box thus becomes a mirror, reflecting your priorities, your values, and the kind of entrepreneur you want to become. It is a navigational tool in the tumultuous seas of entrepreneurship, helping you steer clear of unproductive distractions while guiding you towards your true north.

Everyone operates on a unique circadian rhythm - the natural, internal process that regulates the sleep-wake cycle every 24 hours. By becoming familiar with your rhythm, you can plan tasks accordingly, aligning high-intensity tasks with your peak creative times. Effective time management is not merely about productivity– it is also about ensuring you have enough time to nurture, replenish, and stimulate your creativity. It is about creating intentional spaces in your day for reflection and introspection, for letting your mind wander into uncharted territories, and for exploring the vast, rich landscape of your imagination.

Goal-Setting Strategies for Effective Work

An effectively-crafted goal illuminates your path, providing a beacon of purpose and direction amidst the fog of entrepreneurial ambiguity. Canonical cognitive psychology provides us with valuable insights on goal-setting, illustrating how it directs attention and effort, fosters task persistence and promotes the development of task strategies.

Consider the wisdom of the stoic philosopher Seneca, who wrote: "If one does not know to which port one is sailing, no wind is favorable." His timeless thoughts underscore the role of clear objectives in our journey as creative entrepreneurs. Goals tether our entrepreneurial ship to secure shores, allowing the winds of creativity to propel us in a discernable direction.

It is pertinent to approach goal setting systematically. One of the most compelling yet accessible goal-setting frameworks is the **SMART** mnemonic—an acronym for **Specific, Measurable, Achievable, Relevant,** and **Time-bound**.

A **Specific** goal targets a clear area of improvement or development. As an artist, you could aim to improve your drawing skills or learn a new painting technique. As an entrepreneur, you could strive to increase your client base or expand your brand's social media presence.

Measurable means you must be able to track and measure your progress. This could involve quantifying the number of paintings you wish to complete within a set timeframe or the number of new clients you wish to acquire.

Achievable pertains to the feasibility of your goal. It should stretch your abilities but remain within reach to avoid frustration and disillusionment. Remember, your lighthouse should be attainable on the horizon, not a distant star.

Relevant ensures the goal aligns with your broader ambitions and personal values. If the path illuminated does not lead you towards the entrepreneurial harbor you desire, you need to rethink your route.

Finally, **Time-bound** introduces an element of urgency and encourages accountability. By committing to a timeframe, you facilitate an environment that fosters a sense of responsibility and prevents procrastination.

Incorporating these principles into your goal-setting process can provide a scaffold for your creativity, letting it flourish within a structure that inspires progress rather than stifles it. Imposing self-direction in such a meticulous manner might initially seem antithetical to creative freedom. But herein lies the paradox of goal setting; by shaping our creative efforts with purposeful structure, we liberate ourselves from the chains of uncertainty and heighten our productivity. Goal setting is an interweaving of cognitive psychology and existential philosophy, a nexus where therapy and practical wisdom converge, propelling us on a journey from anxiety to authenticity. We must learn to harness the power of well-crafted goals to guide us on our path to thriving.

Cultivating a Creative Mindset

Creativity requires fertile soil, adequate sunlight, and just the right blend of water and nutrients to grow, blossom, and eventually fruit. The metaphor, though pastoral in its image, captures adequately the essence of what cultivating a creative mindset really entails. A blend of thoughtful tending, tender care, and strategic interventions to maximize the potential of your imaginative prowess.

The first question that emerges is: What does it mean to have a creative mindset? The answer, borrowed from cognitive psychology, is an enabling mental state that encourages associative thinking, curiosity, and the willingness to experiment. It is not merely a reservoir to draw from but akin to the river's ceaseless flow, ever-replenishing and carving new paths of perspective. That said, the key to fostering a creative mindset is understanding its three-tier structure: curiosity, connection, and courage.

Curiosity is the innate spark that triggers exploration. It's the proverbial cat, looking into the unopened box, searching for the unseen. Curiosity is an innate human trait that can be encouraged. Engage your world, immerse yourself in varied experiences; consume art, literature, philosophy, science, culture - anything that piques your interest or challenges your perspective. Embrace novelty and encourage inquisitiveness. Our minds are constantly scanning for new ideas and possibilities. Make it a habit to note them down, no matter how mundane or outlandish they might appear. Some may bear fruit, some may not, yet all add to the compost for future germination.

Connection is the ability to see links between unrelated elements. It's the leap of imagination that bridges gaps, sees patterns and creates novel combinations. Connection, on the other hand, is a cultivated skill. It involves pattern recognition, associative thinking and an active imagination. One way to foster this is through exposure to diverse fields, disciplines, and cultures, cross-pollinating ideas and themes. Another is active contemplation, intentionally taking time to mull over ideas, allowing them to coalesce into unique configurations.

Courage is the trait that keeps fear at bay while we venture into unknown territories of thought and action, it's the audacity to create, knowing full well that failure is an ever-looming possibility. Courage can be the most challenging part of nurturing a creative mindset. Boldly treading uncharted paths or standing by your unique idea amidst skepticism is no small feat. The entrepreneurial world can feel like a constant battle with failure and rejection. However, armed with resilience and self-belief, the creative entrepreneur can find the courage to persevere.

Nurturing a creative mindset is fostering an environment conducive to the birth of ideas, and the boldness to see these ideas to fruition. It is taking the raw clay of thought and bravely molding it into forms that challenge norms, provoke thought, and open up avenues of possibility. Embrace curiosity, foster connections, and invite courage into your mind-garden, and watch as it blossoms into a flourishing orchard of innovation.

Creative Brainstorming Exercises

Delving into the world of creativity and innovation, let us widen our perspective to embrace techniques that can become the catalyst for our entrepreneurial journey. Our minds are our most valuable asset. A prosperously fertile ground where seeds of ideas germinate, grow, and blossom into the flowering of innovation. These ideas, however, don't simply materialize out of thin air; they must be coaxed and nurtured. This nurturing is precisely where creative brainstorming exercises and techniques come into play.

Brainstorming— as an idea generation process— operates on the inherent belief that our mental boundaries crumble when challenged. It invites us to step outside of our well-worn thought patterns, nudging us toward unchartered cerebral territories. It allows us to stretch our thinking capacity, imagining possibilities that may not have been evident within our conventional mindset.

One such technique that has demonstrated effectiveness is mind mapping—a simple yet powerful tool. Essentially, mind mapping is a method used to visually organize information around a central concept—in our case, a central idea or problem. We can utilize mind mapping to brainstorm new ideas, flesh out concepts, and visualize the connections between different elements of our budding enterprises. Think of the central concept as the trunk of a tree with branches that extend outward, each representing a related element or idea. This enables us to view the entirety of our idea as a connected system, bringing clarity, expanding our understanding, and facilitating creative problem solving.

Equally essential to our toolbox is the technique of free writing, wherein we write continuously for a set period—say, fifteen minutes—without focusing on grammar, punctuation, or topic flow. The aim of free writing is to unfetter our internal censor, the voice in our heads that perpetually tells us that our ideas are not good enough. Letting our thoughts flow onto the paper, without self-judgment, we can potentially stumble upon gems of innovative creativity.

Visual ideation is another powerful technique that helps us envision our ideas in tangible forms, enhancing our ability to conceptualize abstract thoughts. Drawing, whether you consider yourself an artist or not, can translate what is complex and intricate in our heads into a visually comprehensible format. Visual ideation encourages us to tap into the often-ignored right side of our brain; it supports us in letting go of the verbal and analytical constraints that sometimes limit our creative juices.

Each of these techniques possesses an individual potential to aid us in venturing beyond our comfort zones, inviting us to dance with the unexpected and embrace the unfamiliar. Embrace them not as rigid rules but as friendly guides—tools to help us explore the vast wilderness of our creative landscapes. Brainstorming isn't a destination but a process. Stay open, stay curious and let your mind wander, for innovation lies not in the paved paths but in the untamed wilderness of exploration.

Boosting Creativity and Productivity

Many creative entrepreneurs grapple with the paradox of creativity and productivity. The former blossoms on uninhibited thinking, dreaming, and experimenting - processes that, in essence, defy strict temporal constraints. On the other hand, productivity thrives on efficiency, organization, and scheduling - aspects that seemingly restrict the fertile realm of creativity. Is this a conundrum where you must inevitably compromise one for the other?

Understand the notion that creativity isn't a sporadic stroke of genius but rather a habit that we can nurture, condition, and refine. Similarly, productivity isn't simply checking off tasks; it's optimizing our time and energy for maximum impact. Understanding this synergistic relationship between creativity and productivity can set the groundwork for a more fruitful entrepreneurial journey. The challenge here lies in the strategic allocation of time and energy to nurture both creativity and productivity. Just as a gardener meticulously plans the landscape, ensuring every plant receives appropriate sunshine, nutrients, and space to thrive, we must craft our schedules to nourish our creative and productive capabilities.

For instance, scheduling regular brainstorming sessions can offer you a playground for your ideas while keeping you on track toward your goals. Isolation of ideas often breeds anxiety; by addressing them collectively in a brainstorming session, you provide an outlet for your creative energy and stimulate mental agility. On the flip side, consider dedicating portions of your day to focused, uninterrupted work. During these periods, put away distractions to improve concentration and harness your productivity. The Pomodoro technique is one such method that balances work intervals with short breaks, fueling sustained attention and preventing cognitive exhaustion.

Reflecting deeply, we uncover connections between our creative tendencies and our mental health. A cluttered mind, weighed down by anxiety and doubt, can stifle our creative spirit. Conversely, nurturing a positive mindset can boost both creativity and productivity. This is where the blend of mindful exercises, as suggested in therapeutic approaches, comes into play - by practicing mindfulness we cultivate a mental space that allows us to navigate thoughts and ideas more efficiently.

Chapter 12: Self-Care Practices for Creative Entrepreneurs

Self-Care Balancing Work and Wellbeing

Self-care is a multidimensional concept that encompasses much more than pampering and indulgence. It is a vital, proactive approach to maintaining health and wellbeing that involves assessing and addressing one's emotional, psychological, physical, and spiritual needs with care, compassion, and intentionality. For creative entrepreneurs who face unique challenges in balancing mental health and business demands, self-care needs to be an essential component of their daily routine and long-term strategy.

The philosopher Socrates famously stated that "an unexamined life is not worth living." this sentiment also applies to your self-care practices. The unexamined life of an artist often leads to burnout, disillusionment, and a stagnation of creativity. By regularly engaging in self-reflection and introspection, you cultivate a deeper understanding of your own needs, desires, and boundaries. This in turn enables you to make more conscious choices about how to allocate your time, energy, and resources in order to achieve a harmonious balance between your personal life and your entrepreneurial endeavors.

In this digital age marked by constant connectivity and information overload, a regular practice of mindfulness is more crucial than ever. Incorporating mindfulness techniques, such as meditation and deep breathing exercises, into your daily routine can help anchor you in the present moment, reduce anxiety, and foster a deeper connection with your inner wisdom. Mindfulness enables you to recognize and respond to stressors in a more balanced, proactive way, allowing you to navigate the challenges of the creative entrepreneurial journey with greater resilience and grace. The old adage "you cannot pour from an empty cup" is particularly relevant for creative entrepreneurs who often pour their heart and soul into their work. In order to maintain the energy, focus, and inspiration required to bring your creative visions to life, it is essential to prioritize activities and experiences that nourish your mind, body, and spirit. This might include engaging in physical exercise, spending time in nature, connecting with loved ones, pursuing personal hobbies or interests, or simply taking time to rest and recharge.

Building Healthy Routines and Boundaries

Boundaries - a simple word yet one fraught with complexity. We encounter this word in an array of contexts, each one reiterating its importance. In therapy, it's a crucial expression of self-respect and protection; in philosophy, it symbolizes the demarcation line between what is and isn't within our power; in the entrepreneurial world, it is the scaffold between chaos and effective management of resources. So then, how do we create these healthy routines and boundaries? The recipe is equal parts **self-knowledge**, **perspective**, and **persistent execution**.

Self-knowledge requires us to ask key questions: What am I capable of? What drains me? What are non-negotiables in my well-being regime? Through this process of inquiry—deep, intentional introspection—we gather the necessary insights to plot out the terrain of our mental landscapes. This is not a stagnant examination; like the ebb and flow of our creativity, our self-knowledge, too, is fluid, evolving with every project, every success, every bout of anxiety or ad-hoc work hurdle. Once furnished with this self-knowledge, we can begin to build. We construct our routines like architects of personal productivity, erecting a structure that houses both our professional and personal aspirations and safeguards our mental health. We create routines that honor our energetic rhythms—ensuring we work during our most productive times and rest when we need to recharge.

Simultaneously, we focus on delineating our boundaries. These are the protective walls that preserve the integrity of our routine, the doors that can be opened or closed to others' demands on our time and energy. An entrepreneur's most precious resource is time; consequently, it must be fiercely protected. If we readily offer time without thought, we may find ourselves depleted and spread thin—an undesirable state for any creative mind. Therefore, we must learn to say no effectively, articulating our boundaries with assertive empathy, appreciating that when we say no to one thing, we're saying yes to something else—often, our own well-being.

However, creating these routines and boundaries isn't enough; we must also commit to implementing them regularly. Routine is less about rigid restriction and more about creating a sustainable rhythm—a dance, not a death march. In the nuanced balance between flexibility and discipline that characterizes effective boundaries and healthy routines, we create a dynamic where our creative mind can thrive. Some people see erecting these boundaries and nurturing these routines as imprisoning creativity. Quite the contrary: we are giving it room to bloom within a protected space. Just as a treasured artwork is framed to highlight its beauty, so too are our life and work framed by these routines and boundaries. They underscore the value we place on our mental health and creative vigor. In our ongoing journey from anxiety to authenticity, their importance cannot be overstated.

Just as we shape our work, so too do we shape our lives. And in the architecting of our daily routines and the setting of firm but thoughtful boundaries, we lay the foundation stones of a life designed for well-being and creativity to thrive together. Each brick set, each hammer strike sounded, takes us one step closer to our goal: a healthy, authentic life, brimming with creative potential.

Mindfulness and Self-Reflection

In an often tumultuous landscape dominated by disruption, innovation, and continuous competition, our minds can become inundated with a relentless bombardment of thoughts, ideas, and anxieties. In the midst of these swirling mental tempests, anchoring our mind in the present moment can seem an insurmountable task. Capturing the symphony of the present moment—can serve as a keystone to a fortified mental state and a flourishing creative wellspring. Indeed, mindfulness is not simply the absence of distraction, but rather a conscious embrace of the present in all its raw and multifaceted beauty. It does not try to banish the thoughts that seep into our conscious experience or suppress the emotions that ripple across our mental seascape. Instead, it invites them in, observes them without judgment or identification, and gently lets them pass, like clouds drifting across a vast sky.

This reflective journey can sometimes prove discomforting as we unearth aspects of ourselves that might be entwined with painful memories, unfulfilled dreams, or latent anxieties. But we must remember this: only by traversing these dark valleys can we scale the illuminated peaks of self-understanding, empathy, and authenticity.

So, how do we blend these valuable practices into our daily lives? A tapestry of techniques exists, from meditation practices such as mindful breathing or body scans to reflective writing in journals or diaries. Other practices might involve spending time in nature, immersed in its infinite patience and quiet resilience, or savoring the beauty of art, teasing apart the threads of shared human experience woven into every melody, brushstroke or word.

Beating Burnout: Sustainable Creativity

As we delve deeper into the core of self-care, we cannot ignore the significant role that burnout plays in the lives of creative entrepreneurs. Burnout is an alarm signaling that the harmony between your work and personal life is off-balance. It underscores an undeniable need to recalibrate and restructure your approach to creativity and business. Burnout, in its raw form, is a state of emotional, mental, and often physical exhaustion brought on by prolonged or recurring stress. For creative entrepreneurs, this stress often stems from an immense pressure to constantly innovate and exceed expectations, while simultaneously managing the practical aspects of running a business.

Overcoming burnout begins with recognizing its symptoms. These are unique to each individual and may include persistent feelings of exhaustion, a lack of enthusiasm for previously enjoyable tasks, and a creeping sense of cynicism or detachment. While these symptoms can be unnerving and even alarming, acknowledging them is the first step towards managing them. Recognize that burnout is not only about your work but about your relationship with yourself and your creative practice. It's important, at this juncture, to not just understand burnout but to employ strategies aimed at preventing and managing it.

One of these strategies involves a conscious effort to respect each aspect of your life and give it the time and energy it deserves. You are not just a creative entrepreneur; you are a multitude of roles and relationships, each deserving focus and care. These boundaries should not only restrict the seamless merging of work and personal life but also guard your mental and emotional wellbeing. It involves saying 'no' when necessary, and implementing discipline in protecting your time and energy.

The third strategy to overcome burnout is to embrace rest. Rest is not a luxury or a reward to be earned; it is a necessity given the nature of your work. Think of rest as a fertile ground that nurtures your creativity and replenishes your enthusiasm. Contrary to popular belief, being dormant is not the opposite of progress; it can often be the catalyst. Overcoming burnout may involve seeking professional help. Therapeutic intervention can provide a structured and guided environment for exploring and managing burnout symptoms. Therapy, in conjunction with a lifestyle focused on maintaining boundaries, can be an effective tool in combating and preventing burnout.

Note that **Burnout does not indicate weakness or inefficacy. On the contrary, it is a testament to the intense passion and dedication you invest in your work**. In the face of burnout, we must remember that we are not infallible, nor should we aspire to be. We are human, complex in our abilities, and subjective in our limits. And it is in this flawed humanity that our authenticity emerges, resolute. In the pursuit of sustainable creativity, may we commit ourselves to understanding our thresholds, prioritizing our wellbeing, seeking support when needed, and appreciating the journey as much as the destination.

Therapeutic Stress Management

From the outset, let's establish a simple truth: stress is not your enemy. Stress is a physiological response, a natural survival instinct. It has been hardwired into our biology to help us navigate dangerous or high-stakes situations. But in the world of creative entrepreneurship, where the dangers are more psychological and societal than physical, unchecked stress can become a burnout catalyst instead of a survival tool. Most of us are well-acquainted with the physical manifestations of stress – a tight chest, a racing heart. When active, it feels like an unwelcome guest interrupting our creative process. Yet, recognizing these manifestations offers us a unique insight, a moment of empowered mindfulness where we can choose to respond rather than react. By integrating therapeutic approaches into your self-care strategies, you can transform your relationship with stress, see it not as a hurdle but as a compass, guiding you towards self-awareness and resilience.

Cognitive Behavioral Therapy presents an effective approach for managing stress. This form of therapy encourages us to challenge our patterns of thought, to question the validity of the negative assumptions we often make under stress. Are you failing or are you learning? Are you being rejected or being redirected? By reframing our perspective, we can transform our mental landscape and nurture a healthier relationship with stress.

Let's take this a notch deeper with the practice of mindfulness. Mindfulness is the act of non-judgmental observation, "being present," often achieved through meditation. It's not about emptying your mind but embracing everything that arises without judgement. When we apply this practice to our stress responses, we create a safe space for understanding and acceptance rather than resistance. Bear in mind that mindfulness is not about immediate resolution but progressive understanding. You're not supposed to "fix" your stress after a ten-minute meditation session. Instead, mindfulness teaches us to observe our stress responses, recognizing them as transient rather than definitive states.

Moving on to the realm of art therapy, it provides yet another breathable space to navigate stress. Art has always held a dual role; it can simultaneously be a form of expression and catharsis. Whether it's drawing, painting, sculpting, or any creative endeavour really, art therapy encourages us to transform our internal turbulence into tangible creations.

Every therapeutic approach offers a different perspective on stress management. Dialectical Behavioural Therapy, for instance, emphasizes the concept of 'distress tolerance'. This approach teaches us to tolerate and accept distressing emotions rather than attempting to immediately change them. It's about being capable of experiencing stress, acknowledging it, and moving forward, regardless of its presence. While these methods work wonders individually, their effectiveness is amplified when integrated into a holistic approach. It's important to remember that therapy is not a one-size-fits-all solution. Each creative entrepreneur has their unique stress responses and coping mechanisms. A blend of therapy, philosophy, and practical wisdom customized to your individual needs crafts the most effective stress management strategy.

Our work often emerges from our emotional depths, making us exceptionally vulnerable to stress. But vulnerability is not weakness. It's strength masked as risk. We can transform our relationship with stress from adversarial to symbiotic. Our creativity, entwined with our mental health, should not be a source of strain in our entrepreneurial journey.

Philosophical Reflections on a Sustainable Creative Lifestyle

In demonstrating unfamiliar perspectives and offering thoughtful, reflective insights about life, philosophy can illuminate deep paths in our shared humanity. In centuries past, philosophers like Aristotle, Confucius, and the stoics extolled the virtues of balance and harmony, principles that remain profound today. Their wisdom offers a robust and profound blueprint for maintaining a balanced and sustainable creative lifestyle. This balance is not merely an equilibrium of time between work and leisure. In its deepest sense, it is an internal harmony of mental, emotional, and physical wellbeing. Such harmony fuels not just our creative endeavors, but also our overall experience of life.

For the creative entrepreneur, overindulgence in work can lead to burnout, while excessive leisure might result in lethargy and lack of motivation. It's Aristotle's doctrine of the "golden mean" that encourages us to find a moderate position between deficiency and excess—a haven of balance where creativity and wellness dance in synchrony.

Confucius, too, offers an insightful lens for viewing balance. He speaks of 'Zhong Yong' or Doctrine of the Mean, which encourages us to embrace moderation and centrism in all aspects of life. For the creative mind, this philosophy translates into equilibrium in inspiration and execution— we must allow ample time for both the birth of ideas and their manifestation in our work.

Meanwhile, Stoicism—an ancient philosophy embraced by thinkers such as Seneca and Marcus Aurelius—proffers the concept of the "indifference of externals". According to the stoics, the key to composure amidst turmoil is understanding that we cannot control everything. We can, however, govern our reactions to them. This principle arms the creative entrepreneur with fortitude in the face of volatile markets, fluctuating trends, or critical feedback.

In contemplating these ancient yet timeless concepts in the modern world of creative entrepreneurship, we create a foundational basis for mental resilience. We begin to perceive our business not as an all-consuming entity but as an integral part of our larger existence.

Chapter 13: Breaking Free from Comparison Traps

Comparison Traps in Historical Perspective

Standing on the shoulders of giants, as the saying goes, implies a vantage point that holds tremendous inspiration, but also the potential for debilitating comparison. Artists throughout history have found themselves in this predicament, often wrestling with the deeply personal experience of creating and the inevitable comparisons to others' creations.

Consider the life of Vincent van Gogh. Though his work has posthumously achieved widespread acclaim, during his lifetime, he struggled to escape the shadows of his contemporaries. Van Gogh was consistently plagued by feelings of inferiority, frequently comparing his work unfavorably to that of other artists. He was a man who, despite the eventual recognition of his transcendental talent, found himself perennially submerged in the shadows of his contemporaries. Van Gogh lived in an era where artistic innovation was admired and sought after, yet his innovative style was often disregarded, leaving him hidden in the peripheries of the art world. Van Gogh's life was marred by a constant and unnerving struggle with feelings of inferiority. His comparison of his own work to that of other artists was frequent, a painstaking process that left him feeling hopelessly inadequate in the face of their work. He would spend countless hours poring over their pieces, scrutinizing every last detail, and measuring it against his own. This persistent comparison wasn't without its ramifications; it gnawed at his confidence, gradually eroding his belief in his own abilities. This painful comparison trap not only impaired his self-esteem but also significantly affected his mental health. Yet, it's astounding how his profound struggle gave birth to some of the most iconic artwork the world has ever experienced.

Another poignant example lies in the life of the American poet and novelist Sylvia Plath, a literary maven whose legacy is defined by the depth of her anguish and the brilliance of her craft, often straddling the line between genius and despair, and remains a captivating figure in American literature. She was born in Boston, Massachusetts, in 1932, to Otto Plath, a German immigrant, and Aurelia Schober Plath, a first-generation American of Austrian descent. From an early age, Sylvia demonstrated an innate talent for writing, and the fusion of her rich heritage and upbringing in America provided a unique backdrop for her growing literary voice. The complexities of her personal life, marked by her father's death when she was just eight years old and a series of romantic entanglements in her formative years, became rich fodder for her work. Often, her poems and prose shifted between profound melancholia and euphoric creativity, embodying the paradox of her existence. In the years when she was forging her path in the literary world, she found herself often juxtaposed against her contemporaries, their successes serving as a yardstick against which she measured her own accomplishments. Plath was intermittently haunted by feelings of inadequacy, a sense that she was eternally overshadowed by the literary heavyweights of her time. This constant fixation on comparison and competition bore heavily on her, exerting a crippling pressure that threatened to stifle her creative spirit. The burden of this unmet expectation cast a gloomy pall on her bright and promising career. The vicissitude of her personal life, her struggles with mental health issues, and the constant comparison to her contemporaries began to rob her of the joy derived from her craft, transforming her writing into a bittersweet catharsis of her inner turmoil.

Venturing closer to our era, Quentin Tarantino, an avant-garde filmmaker known for his idiosyncratic narrative style and use of violence as a storytelling tool, never shied away from expressing his anxiety over being compared to his esteemed predecessors. Born in Knoxville, Tennessee, on March 27, 1963, Tarantino was raised by his mother in Los Angeles, California. His passion for movies was ignited at a young age when he would find solace in the local theaters, a practice that ultimately influenced his unique and non-linear storytelling approach in filmmaking. Despite the accolades and worldwide recognition that his work has earned, including two Academy Awards, Tarantino has never been immune to the insecurities that often plague artists. He has always been candid about his feelings of inadequacy and the pressure that comes with being compared to iconic filmmakers such as Martin Scorsese or Stanley Kubrick. In an interview with a prominent film magazine, Tarantino once confessed, "When you're a film director, you're in a constant battle with your own inflated expectations." This sentiment encapsulates the essence of his constant struggle to outdo himself, a reflection of his relentless pursuit of artistic perfection. Despite his celebrated status in the industry, the comparison trap lurked, looming large in his creative process. His anxiety was not just limited to being compared to his contemporaries, but also extended to his earlier, critically acclaimed works like "Pulp Fiction" or "Reservoir Dogs". Every new project came with the daunting task of meeting or exceeding the high standards set by his previous films, a challenge that was both motivating and intimidating for him. Tarantino's apprehension is a testament to the relentless pressure that artists face in their careers, constantly being measured against their past successes and the accomplishments of others in their field.

These historical instances serve as stark reminders that comparison traps are not exclusive to an era, medium, or individual artistic temperament. They highlight a pervasive issue common in the creative life-cycle; one that can be intensely damaging if left unchecked. Comparison, in its unhealthy form, can morph into a debilitating adversary, distorting our perception of self-worth and impairing our creative expression. Though these artists' lived experiences might not exactly mirror our own, their struggles deliver insights. Their narratives underline the importance of overcoming comparison traps, fostering a healthy perspective towards individual creativity, and bolstering our mental resilience.

In the realm of invention where ideas are currency, it's natural to measure one's worth against the scales of external benchmark. However, it is crucial to recognize that this form of comparison can hamper our creativity and hinder our progress. Breaking these comparison traps requires acknowledging their existence and understanding their impact. It's about realigning focus away from what others are doing and redirecting it towards our unique creative journey. It is not an easy shift, but it is an essential one.

Embracing Individuality in the Creative Journey

The path you chose as a creative entrepreneur is not a well-trodden one. It is branching and unpredictable, often wavering, twisting, and turning with each creative venture. You, my friend, are a pioneer in your unique realm of creativity. This path of yours is exclusive to you, woven from individual threads of your experiences, insights, comforts, discomforts, delights, and despairs. Philosophy urges us to comprehend this individuality and embrace it, for it is the basis upon which you construct your creative enterprise.

Let's turn to ancient philosophy for a clearer picture. The great Stoic philosopher Epictetus once proclaimed, "Only the educated are free." This assertion encompasses more than formal education; it speaks to the learning we garner through exploring the intricate corridors of our minds. It refers to the liberation attained from comprehending our own uniqueness and fostering it, brushed away from society's conforming and rigid iron strokes. Acknowledge that you are not just creating a business; you are creating a world—a world painted with the hues of your experiences, shaped with the curves and angles of your worldview. Your ventures are but outer manifestations of this inner world. Yet, the creative journey isn't isolated from the external world. It interfaces with the market, the consumers, the critics. However, the true essence of your creativity does not lie in this interface but in the unique world that you cultivate within. Each landmark in your entrepreneurial journey should be more than a check on a list; it should be a revelation of yourself, an unveiling of an aspect of your world.

That is not to say that the practicalities of the world should be disregarded. An Italian philosopher, Niccolò Machiavelli, brilliantly advised, "Entrepreneurs are simply those who understand that there is little difference between obstacle and opportunity and can turn both to their advantage." Our objective is not to isolate ourselves from the world but rather to navigate it using our own compass, which we calibrate according to our individuality. It is undoubtedly daunting to behold the vast, unfamiliar terrain of your journey. Still, the footing beneath you is solid, rooted in the ground of your individuality.

As we continue on this individual journey, I'll leave you with the words of famed poet Robert Frost: "Two roads diverged in a wood, and I—I took the one less traveled by, And that has made all the difference." Your path, the one less traveled, is not easy. It is marked by brambles of self-doubt and pitfalls of failure. But it is yours, made not by the steps of others but by your own. And that will make all the difference.

Therapeutic Perspectives on Managing Comparison Struggles

The human propensity for comparison is powerful, deep-rooted, and often relentless. We exist in a world of relativity, constantly comparing our life, work, abilities, and accomplishments to those around us. How does one maintain the strength of self-belief amid inevitable waves of comparison? Reflecting on the psychotherapist Carl Rogers, he posited, "The only person who is educated is the one who has learned how to learn and change." This notion of resilience through learning applies directly to managing the struggles sparked by comparison.

At the heart of any therapeutic approach to such struggles is the concept of self-awareness. It provides us with both a shield and a lens - a shield from the harmful impact of unhealthy comparison and a lens to view our unique journey with perspective and grace.

Psychotherapist Albert Ellis's Rational Emotive Behaviour Therapy (REBT), a form of cognitive behavioural therapy, offers a pragmatic approach that could prove significantly beneficial. It places considerable emphasis on identifying and combatting irrational beliefs, many of which stem from the dangerous act of comparison. Consider the belief, "If I am not the very best, I am nothing." In the creative realm, this can manifest itself when your work is not recognized or eclipsed by others'. By disassembling this belief through REBT techniques, you will likely realize its irrationality and reframe your thought process.

While comparison struggles are not eradicated overnight, these therapeutic perspectives contribute towards managing and eventually minimizing their impact. Comparisons may be inevitable, but they need not be paralyzing. It's in this realization, this shift of perspective, where you begin to reclaim control of your creative journey. It's here, that you start to break free from the constraints of comparison, welcoming a more undisturbed, authentic creative flow in your entrepreneurial voyage. This is less a destination, but more an ongoing, evolving journey; you are not merely coping anymore but thriving, from the shackles of anxiety to the solace of authenticity.

Self-Acceptance and Uniqueness: Practical Exercises

As we turn the page of this chapter, embracing the journey of self-awareness, let's delve into the practical application. These exercises are designed with the intent to help creative entrepreneurs like you cultivate self-acceptance and celebrate the uniqueness that underscores the very fabric of their creative expression.

Exercise 1: The Mirror Exercise — The mirror can be an object of introspection, a vehicle for unmasking our deep-seated unease, or it can serve as a tool for critical self-exploration. The mirror exercise is simple, yet transformative. Stand in front of a mirror and look at yourself – not just your physical self, but also the embodiment of your journey, your thoughts, your fears, and your brilliance. Now, voice out loud what you see. Note the mistakes, but also the triumphs. Recognize the anxiety, but also the strength. This exercise aims to foster self-acceptance through radical honesty, thereby aiding you to not only accept but cherish every facet of your creative individuality.

Exercise 2: The Affirmation Mantra — The power of language is monumental. Crafting a personalized affirmation mantra plays a significant role in fostering a positive image of the self. First, identify the areas in which you often find yourself lost in the comparison trap. Next, create an affirmation that counters this negative thought pattern and promotes self-worth. For example, if your comparison trap is routinely feeling less innovative than other entrepreneurs, your affirmation could be: "My creativity is unique, and my ideas have value". Repeat this mantra to yourself, especially during moments of self-doubt. Repeating these words of affirmation can establish a healthier, more positive dialogue with your creative self.

Exercise 3: The Uniqueness Journal — Maintaining a uniqueness journal serves as a continuous reminder of your one-of-a-kind personal and creative journeys. Dedicate a few minutes at the end of each day to write about something unique you did, thought, or experienced. This could range from a creative idea that popped into your mind, a project you started, a book passage that moved you, a conversation that felt inspiring, or even the distinct way you brew your morning coffee. By mindfully acknowledging these daily instances of individuality, you cultivate an environment where your unique traits are not merely accepted but celebrated.

Exercise 4: The Art of Being Alone — Spending quality time with oneself can be a particularly enlightening experience for creative entrepreneurs. Carve out a dedicated "me" time in your schedule, without the distractions of work, social media, or societal norms. Use this solitude to engage in activities that fuel your soul and creativity, to think profoundly, to reflect, or simply to be. When you spend time with yourself, you will gain a deeper understanding and acceptance of your unique traits, and paving the way for self-acceptance.

Each exercise taps into different aspects of your journey towards self-acceptance and self-celebration. This journey is an ongoing process, but remember, in this process, you are not alone. Each creative entrepreneur grapples with their distinct struggles and triumphs in their path, and accepting and celebrating your authentic self is the cornerstone of a fulfilling entrepreneurial journey.

Embrace these exercises, honour our unique spirit, and radiate authenticity. For, it is only when we recognize and celebrate our individuality can we truly shine in our entrepreneurial endeavors, unfettered by comparison traps. Remember, the world needs your unique creative spark. So hone it, cherish it, and flaunt it unabashedly.

Chapter 14: Therapy Toolbox for Creative Minds

Tailored Therapies for Creative Entrepreneurship

While the notion of 'therapy' often triggers the mental image of a serene, dimly lit space with a psychologist patiently awaiting your arrival, in reality, therapeutic tools and techniques are not confined to such conventional settings. They are, in fact, subtle but valuable resources that can greatly enhance our daily living, and more specifically, our creative outputs. The mind is our primary working tool, our most prized asset. Thus, ensuring its optimal functioning is paramount to our success. This subchapter provides you with a toolkit, a set of practical therapeutic options curated with a unique focus on the challenges and demands of creative entrepreneurship.

1. Mindfulness-Based Stress Reduction (MBSR) — Mindfulness is a shared language between the spheres of mental health and creativity. It is a state of active, open attention to the present, which can irrigate the fertile soil of your imagination. MBSR, a program designed by Jon Kabat-Zinn, advocates for a heightened awareness of one's thoughts, feelings, and body sensations in day-to-day life. It has been extensively researched with demonstrated benefits in reducing stress and promoting wellbeing. Regularly practicing MBSR can not only mitigate the adverse effects of entrepreneurial stress but also cultivate an alertness to the stirrings of creativity within you.

2. Cognitive Behavioral Techniques (CBT) — Cognitive-behavioral techniques are a staple in many therapists' toolkits and can be particularly beneficial to creative entrepreneurs. They work on the principle that our thought patterns influence our feelings and actions. If we can effectively challenge and change harmful cognitive distortions, we can foster healthier behaviors and emotional states. Creative individuals often grapple with 'cognitive traps' such as perfectionism or catastrophizing, which may hamper their productivity. CBT allows you to identify these cognitive distortions, question their validity, and replace them with healthier, more balanced thoughts.

3. Grounding Techniques — In the midst of a whirlwind of creative ideas or the stress of an impending deadline, we can sometimes lose touch with our present reality. Grounding techniques help to anchor us back into the 'here and now' by focusing on our direct sensory experiences. This could be as simple as focusing on your breath, the feeling of your feet against the floor, or the taste of your morning coffee. These practices can provide a healthy balance by pulling us back from the often volatile terrain of our creative and entrepreneurial minds.

4. Journaling — When considering therapeutic tools, never underestimate the power of a pen and a blank sheet of paper. Journaling can provide an outlet for emotions that may stifle creativity or contribute to anxiety. It is a space where thoughts can be raw, unedited, and free from external judgment. Moreover, the act of writing can itself be a catalyst for creativity, often unearthing hidden treasures buried deep within your subconscious.

5. Relaxation Techniques — Relaxation practices such as progressive muscle relaxation, guided imagery, and deep breathing exercises can help to alleviate stress and rejuvenate the creative mind. A relaxed state supports optimal brain functioning and can bolster the generation of innovative ideas.

Being a creative entrepreneur involves continuous tapping into your mental and emotional resources. While this can be demanding, the tools provided in this chapter serve as mental health aids to help you come ou. Like any tool, they are most effective when used regularly, and results may not be immediately apparent. Yet, as you weave these practices into your daily life, you will find yourself moving closer to a state of balance between stress and serenity, creating an environment where both you and your creative business can flourish.

Techniques for Stress Management

Here, we will briefly explore a variety of practical tools that can help creative entrepreneurs effectively manage stress and build resilience.

1. Mindfulness Meditation: Powerful technique for managing stress is mindfulness meditation. By practicing mindful awareness, we can cultivate a greater sense of calm and focus, allowing us to navigate challenges with clarity and resilience. During mindfulness meditation, we intentionally bring our attention to the present moment, observing our thoughts and feelings without judgment. This practice helps us develop a greater awareness of our stress triggers and empowers us to respond to them in a more intentional and compassionate manner.

2. Breathwork: In moments of stress, our breath can be a powerful tool for grounding and centering ourselves. By consciously focusing on our breath and engaging in deep, intentional breathing, we activate the body's relaxation response. This simple yet effective practice can quickly reduce stress levels and create space for clarity and renewed energy. Incorporating breathwork exercises into our daily routine can help us proactively manage stress and prevent burnout.

3. Progressive Muscle Relaxation: Progressive muscle relaxation is a technique that involves systematically tensing and releasing different muscle groups in the body. By intentionally tensing and then relaxing each muscle group, we can release physical tension and experience a deep sense of relaxation. This practice not only relieves stress but also promotes a greater mind-body connection, allowing us to be more attuned to our bodies' signals and needs.

4. Creative Expression: We have a unique advantage when it comes to managing stress – our creative outlets. Engaging in a creative practice, whether it's painting, writing, playing music, or any other form of self-expression, can serve as a powerful stress relief tool. Creative expression allows us to channel our emotions, release tension, and find solace in the act of creation itself. By making time for our creative pursuits, we not only nurture our well-being but also tap into a wellspring of inspiration and rejuvenation.

By incorporating these therapeutic techniques into our daily lives, we can effectively manage stress and prevent burnout in the creative field. Building a toolbox of self-care practices and making them a priority can empower us to navigate the challenges of creative entrepreneurship with resilience, authenticity, and well-being. In the next subchapter, we will explore exercises for enhancing self-awareness and fostering a positive mindset, further equipping creative entrepreneurs with the tools they need to thrive.

Exercises for Improving Self-Awareness and a Positive Mindset

Firstly, I invite you to delve into the labyrinth of your self-perception. Through reflection, begin to distinguish your thoughts, emotions, and behaviors. An excellent method to facilitate these reflections is to maintain a journal. This endeavor, often described as the 'mirror of the mind,' aids in documenting your thoughts, capturing your emotions, and recording your behaviors. This can be a digital journal, each entry can indeed serve as the artist's brush, forming a vivid portrait of your internal state. It helps you pinpoint patterns, unravel repressed feelings, and even voice anxieties. Alternatively, the act of articulating your fears can sideline anxiety, reducing its towering stature to manageable proportions and freeing from your mind, now that it exists on a physical location.

My second recommendation is a practice called 'mindful awareness'. Being present, being 'here,' is a skill that can be honed through deliberate practice. Some consider it an art, others a science, but universally, it illuminates our path towards enriching self-awareness. Mindful awareness involves focusing on the present moment, accepting it without judgment, and embracing it in all its entirety. When we practice mindful awareness during our creative processes, we immerse ourselves fully in the act of creation. This immersion allows us to savor every thought that sparks our creativity and every emotion that fuels our passion. Fascinatingly, this simple act of presence can lead you to discover new insights about your creative process and habits.

Lastly, let us consider the cognitive exercises for positivity. It is essential to understand that the glass is half full and half empty. Yet, we control the narrative. We hold the power to shift our focus towards abundance or scarcity; we can concentrate on our accomplishments or fixate on our inadequacies. Cognitive exercises such as positive affirmation and visualization can aid in fostering a positive mindset. As we feed the mind with positive thoughts and images, we slowly nudge it towards a more optimistic perspective—one that fuels inspiration rather than a crippling fear.

This triad of exercises—journaling, mindful awareness, and cognitive positivity practices—are potent tools in your psychotherapy toolbox. I urge you to regularly engage in these exercises. Create your mental space for them, just like you would for your creative work. Let these practices be your steady companion on your creative journey. And remember, the journey towards self-awareness is not linear— it meanders, halts, and sometimes even reverses. Embrace these fluctuations with compassion and patience.

Chapter 15: Resilience in Uncertain Times: Thriving Through Challenges

Embracing Life's Challenges

The unyielding hands of time, the unforgiving pendulums of circumstances, and the relentless uncertainty of existence – these elements comprise the theater of life where we perform. Notably, the artist-entrepreneur commands a unique spotlight on this stage. The ancient art of questioning and understanding the human condition can illuminate our path through this dance. It offers invaluable insights to the creative entrepreneur navigating uncertain times. Philosophy, in its wisdom, urges us to view our tribulations not as insurmountable obstacles but as opportunities for growth.

Consider Seneca's wisdom, a leading figure in Stoicism, a philosophy practiced by great minds across the centuries – from ancient emperors to contemporary entrepreneurs. Seneca's words echo through millennia, "We suffer more often in imagination than in reality." Anxiety, whether about our artistic endeavors or entrepreneurial ventures, often stems from the fear of confronting an imagined future - one that is painted with the darkest hues of our apprehensions. Reflected in Seneca's teachings is an understanding that worry, in essence, is a surplus of creativity misdirected towards envisioning catastrophe rather than progress. As creatives we have the power to harness this surplus creativity and direct it towards constructive avenues. Through this, we discipline our minds to adapt to challenges and to thrive amidst uncertainty.

Moreover, the serenity found in the Eastern philosophies of Buddhism and Taoism present a compelling perspective. For instance, they teach us the importance of emotional equipoise and mindful presence. The artistry of entrepreneurship mirrors the rhythmic ebb and flow of nature, characterized by constant change. Just as a tree withstands storm and sun alike by yielding and adapting, so too must the entrepreneurial artist adopt resilience. By grounding ourselves in the present and maintaining an open, adaptive mindset, we can weather any storm and manifest our visions into reality. The entrepreneurial journey may not always echo our carefully sketched blueprints. It will take surprising turns, halting stops, and unexpected leaps. However, the philosophy's emphasis on adapting teaches us to perceive these not as setbacks but as setups for the next leap forward. It is a transformative perspective, encouraging us to see each hurdle not as a stumbling block but as a stepping-stone leading us towards our authentic selves.

Therapeutic Strategies for Uncertainty and Ambiguity

Often, anxiety stems from our fear of the unknown. As creators, we can find ourselves spiralling into a vortex of endless "whatifs" and hypothetical scenarios, clouding our mental space and inhibiting our creative process. To navigate uncertainty, we need to acknowledge the existence of this fear and then tune into a healing stance. Cognitive Behavioural Therapy(CBT), for instance, prompts us to challenge these fears objectively. It encourages us to question the probability of our fears manifesting and redirect our focus on our strengths and past victories. By adopting CBT techniques, we actively engage our analytical brain, tempering the emotional surge that often accompanies uncertainty. Simultaneously, we counteract tendencies towards catastrophic thinking, allowing a more balanced perspective of our situation. Through gradually shifting our mindset to rationalise fear, we not only reduce the intensity of anxiety but anchor ourselves in the present, fostering a nurturing environment for creativity to flourish.

The realm of ambiguity, on the other hand, is where clarity blurs, and answers are not definitive. It is a sea often stirred by the winds of the entrepreneurial journey. Whether deciding on the direction of a new project or interpreting feedback from peers or clients, ambiguity can generate a whirlpool of indecision and doubt. To navigate this uncharted territory, strategies such as mindfulness-based interventions (MBIs) have been proven effective. Mindfulness, as practiced in MBIs, allows us to sit comfortably in the ambiguity without feeling overwhelmed. It encourages acceptance of the unknown, and it cultivates an environment for innate wisdom to surface. When we strip back the pressures to have all the answers, we allow ourselves the grace to be human, to stumble, make mistakes, and most importantly, to learn. It's in this space that we experience the freedom to create without constraints and to explore new artistic realms, uncharted by our previous fears.

Moreover, applying the principles of Acceptance and Commitment Therapy (ACT) can further bolster our mental resilience amidst ambiguity. ACT teaches us to acknowledge our feelings without judgment and to commit to actions that align with our values. Here, ambiguity ceases to be a roadblock and instead becomes a catalyst for growth. We learn to welcome the unknown, using it as an opportunity to delve deeper into our creative selves and express authenticity in our work.

Therapeutic strategies provide us with lasting tools to face these challenges. By utilizing CBT, MBIs, and ACT as navigational beacons, we can transform our perception of these obstacles. No longer are they enormous, overbearing stones blocking our path but instead stepping stones—albeit occasionally slippery—that can aid in our progression towards becoming resilient creative entrepreneurs.

History, Creativity and Adversity

The life of Ludwig van Beethoven, the iconic composer, is a testament to this. Despite grappling with traumatic childhood experiences and irreparable hearing loss in his late twenties, Beethoven channeled his hardships into his music. His compositions, imbued with his personal struggle, resonated with audiences, transcending the barriers of time and space.

Pondering Beethoven's story, we glean an essential principle: Creativity can transform personal struggle into collective triumph. His resilience amidst adversity reminds us to harness our own challenges as fertile ground for our innovative endeavors.

Another beacon of resilience shines from the world of literature - Maya Angelou. Angelou endured a life marked by racial discrimination, poverty, and traumatic abuse. Yet, she leveraged these experiences to pen profound narratives, addressing themes of social injustice and personal healing that echoed through reading cultures globally. Angelou didn't just survive; she used her voice to transform struggle into strength, pain into poetry. Gleaning insights from her story, we learn the power of authentic voice and vulnerability in reaching a larger audience. Her resilience encourages us to embrace our unique journey, using even its harshest elements as building blocks for our entrepreneurial growth.

Fast-forwarding to contemporary times, we find Steve Jobs, a name synonymous with innovative entrepreneurship. Jobs faced numerous business challenges and multiple failures, including being fired from his own company. Yet, these setbacks didn't diminish his spirit. Instead, he used these experiences as springboards for creating groundbreaking technology and reshaping the digital landscape. Jobs' tale encapsulates an entrepreneurial truth - that failure is not an end but a redirection, an opportunity for growth and rerouting towards success. His resilience in the face of business adversity inspires us to view our own entrepreneurial failures not as terminal judgments but as stepping stones towards innovation.

In understanding this, we empower ourselves with the belief that we, too, can mold our challenges into opportunity, that we can manifest resilience in the face of uncertainty.

Chapter 16: Building Resilient Relationships in the Creative Community

Fostering Collaborative Relationships

In the journey of creative entrepreneurship, one does not travel alone. A supportive network of relationships—both personal and professional—provides a much-needed grounding force, a source of inspiration, and a lifeline in times of struggle. As a creative entrepreneur, building resilient relationships isn't just a valuable endeavor—it's a necessary one.

The first principle to fostering these relationships is, quite simply, empathy. This means stepping out of one's own perspective and striving to understand the feelings, thoughts, and experiences of those around you. Recognizing the value of another person's ideas, acknowledging their concerns and striving to relate with their experiences can serve as a compelling adhesive in any relationship. This reciprocity of emotional understanding forms the bedrock of any strong and resilient connection.

The second principle involves nurturing trust. Be it colleagues, mentors or clients, the foundation of any lasting relationship is trust. Trusting someone implies that you believe in their consistency, and in return, they believe in yours. In this reciprocal process, your authenticity plays a crucial role. The more genuine you are, the easier it becomes for others to trust your actions and intentions.

Our third principle is embodying respect. Every individual you encounter in your entrepreneurial journey is a unique mosaic of experiences, skills, talents, and quirks. Each person has something valuable to offer, whether through their insights, their perspectives, or their ability to challenge and push you towards growth. Respecting this individuality, in turn, intensifies the richness of your creative work.

This brings us to the fourth principle: active engagement. It is easy to become consumed by our work, neglecting to nurture the relationships that support us in the process. Active engagement involves acknowledging the importance of those around you and investing time and energy in maintaining those connections. This could be as simple as a coffee catch-up, a brainstorming session, or even a quick message expressing your appreciation.

Lastly, fostering supportive relationships requires adaptability. Relationships evolve, just like us, and being adaptable means that we allow those relationships to grow, to morph without stifling them. Adaptability involves understanding that not every relationship will remain the same, and that's okay. In fact, it's more than okay—it's a testament to growth, both yours and theirs. Building resilient relationships is a dynamic process, by practicing empathy, fostering trust, embodying respect, actively engaging, and embracing adaptability, we create a web of connections that not only support our creative journey but enrich it along the way. It is through these connections that we gather the collective strength to navigate the waters of creative entrepreneurship, transforming our anxieties into authenticity, and our struggles into success.

Addressing Challenges Through Communication

The thought of managing such interpersonal challenges within the creative sphere might induce an anxiety surge. In these moments, it is essential to remember that we have a potent therapeutic tool at our disposal: communication. It has the power to mend, bridge, decode, and clarify, ultimately becoming the key to navigating interpersonal challenges adroitly. Therapeutically applied, communication begins with understanding. Understanding that each person we interact with carries their unique worldview and emotional template. Our creative ideas may not resonate with everyone, and that's not just acceptable—it's healthy. Art thrives in diversity, in the clash and convergence of different perspectives.

As a contemplative writing exercise, try listing down instances where you encountered interpersonal challenges within your creative interactions. Could they have been stemmed or resolved with more effective communication? Reflecting on these scenarios can provide insight into our communication patterns and how they affect our interpersonal relationships. Adopting a strategic yet empathetic approach to communication can defuse tension, reduce anxiety, and foster mutual understanding. Start by creating a safe space for dialogue—be it in person, over a call, or even in an email exchange. This safe communication space calls for active listening, a therapeutic technique that requires us to be fully present and engaged when the other person is speaking.

Active listening involves tuning into what the speaker is expressing emotionally and not just verbally. It's about understanding their perspective, empathizing with their feelings—even if they seem to contradict our own. This genuine interest in their viewpoint encourages openness and vulnerability, leading to a more profound connection. In the creative realm, where ideas are as diverse as the stars in the sky, conflicts are inevitable. However, these conflicts do not have to result in fractured relationships or stunted creativity. A disagreement over a creative project can be turned into an opportunity for innovation, push boundaries, and stimulate growth—provided we embrace therapeutic communication techniques.

One such technique is nonviolent communication (NVC), developed by psychologist Marshall Rosenberg. NVC is a method that stresses empathy, authenticity, and constructive conflict resolution. It can be particularly helpful in navigating disagreements within the creative realm. In its essence, NVC involves expressing how we feel, what we need, and how we might meet those needs without using blame, criticism, or demands. It's rooted in understanding and respect for ourselves and others. Take a moment to ponder how this strategy could be implemented in your creative interactions. Consider instances of conflict or tension and imagine applying NVC: addressing your feelings and needs, understanding the other person's standpoint, finding common ground, and collaboratively working towards conflict resolution.

On this journey from anxiety to authenticity, the navigation of interpersonal challenges is a fundamental cornerstone. By weaving therapeutic communication strategies into our interactions, we not only fortify our relationships but also build a resilient creative community. As we enhance our communication skills, we unlearn the fear associated with disagreements and critiques, leading to lesser anxiety and higher creative productivity. Remember—our art may be subjective, but the effort to understand should always be intentional.

Networking Tips for Building a Creative Community

The process of networking in the creative world is as much a game of strategy as it is a dance with cogitation. It requires a thoughtful and deliberate balance of presence, communication, and mutual collaboration. The endeavor to build your creative community begins with a profound understanding of the value of each connection you make. Human nature compels us to lean towards individuals who share our interests, values, and creative inclinations. However, networking isn't simply about aligning with those of similar destinations; it's about intertwining journeys. Look for individuals who complement your creative style and thought processes, as well as those who challenge them. Each person you meet is a potential catalyst for innovation and expansion of your creative repertoire. Treat each interaction with respect and be genuinely interested in what others have to say. In this industry, currency lies in ideas, and every conversation is a potential goldmine. Active listening, a therapeutic communication technique, can be advantageous here. This isn't a business transaction; it's an exchange of creative energies.

Resilience of a creative community lies in its nurtured diversity and inclusivity. The collective strength of a group is not merely sum of its parts; it's the product of shared efforts, diverse perspective and collaborative growth. Networking also extends to professional spheres. Social media platforms are rife with opportunities to connect with creative minds globally, offering an ever-widening adaptable network. Engage with content that inspires you, start conversations, and build relationships beyond geographic constraints. The consistent use of these platforms for linkage can have prolific effects on your creative engagement.

The creative community also thrives on reciprocity. As much as you may seek inspiration and support, be willing to offer the same to others. This not only amplifies the essence of communal creativity but also enforces an empathy-driven supportive environment. Collaborative projects, critiques, resources sharing, or just simple encouragement can fortify your place within this community, making it resilient in its unity. There's strength in numbers, and a resilient creative community can act as a buffer against the often turbulent tides of the artistic journey and entrepreneurial hardship. However, it isn't a structure to hide behind but a resource to draw from, a reservoir of collective wisdom, creative inspiration, and reliable camaraderie.

Chapter 17: Mindful Marketing: Authenticity in Promotion

Authentic Marketing

In the ocean of branded voices and saturated markets, how does a creative entrepreneur remain consistently true to their essence while striving to be heard above the waves? The answer lies in mindful marketing. The core of mindful marketing is authenticity in promotion. Our journey through the intricate labyrinth of creative entrepreneurship has led us to this point, where our reflections have bred resilience, our struggles have fostered strength, and our authenticity has begun to commandeer our artistic endeavours. Here, at the intersection of creativity and business, of vision and promotion, we find mindful marketing.

Understanding mindful marketing requires us to revisit the realm of authenticity we explored in earlier chapters. Authenticity in this context refers to maintaining a genuine, consistent, and relatable representation of oneself or one's brand in the realm of promotion. It is the audacious act of allowing your true self or your brand's unique identity to shine through in your marketing strategies, unhindered by societal expectations or market demands. You see, marketing and creativity aren't adversaries engaged in a perpetual tug-of-war. In fact, they are partners. While marketing has often been painted as a necessary evil in the creative pursuit—an operation that seemingly demands a certain level of counterfeit to thrive—it can actually serve as an extension of your artistic expression when done mindfully.

I invite you to ponder over it from an existentialist lens. Recall Jean-Paul Sartre's assertion that "existence precedes essence" — the notion that we first exist, then construct our essence by our choices, actions, and their consequences. Now, apply this existentialist tenet to marketing. Isn't promoting your work merely another facet of existing as a creative entrepreneur? And by being mindful and authentic in your marketing efforts, aren't you further sculpting your essence and shaping your creative identity? **Consider, for a moment, the idea of an artist's 'signature style'. Explicit or implied, it is a fusion of both conscious and subconscious choices they've made throughout their creative journey.** This stylistic embodiment is their authentic and unique voice, their essence, woven into the fabric of their work. Now, let's extrapolate this to marketing. Your promotional strategies should be a harmonious extension of this signature style, channelling the same energy, ethos, and essence.

Mindful marketing eschews the mechanistic approach of conventional sales dynamics. Instead, it endorses a holistic perspective. The primary drive here isn't selling for the sake of selling but creating a meaningful connection – a sense of resonance – with your audience. It's about inviting your audience to engage with your work on an emotional, intellectual, and even spiritual level. It's about using your promotional platforms not as billboards for cold selling but as stages for amplifying your authentic voice. The beauty of authenticity in promotion lies in its transformative potential. By practising mindful marketing, you don't merely sell a product or a service; you share a piece of your creation. You do not just create customers; you cultivate a community. You don't just generate revenue; you build relationships. Authentic promotion encourages your audience to look beyond your brand's commercial value and connect. Mindful marketing offers an opportunity to assert your individuality, to rise above the sea of sameness. By being authentic in your promotion, you not only establish a distinctive identity but also attract an audience that appreciates and resonates with your unique approach.

As entrepreneurs, we are not merely trade operators. We are innovators. We are visionaries. We are storytellers. We have the power to transform mundane marketing strategies into meaningful narratives, commercial promotions into candid conversations. We can replace the disingenuous noise of traditional salesmanship with the harmonious melody of our authentic voice. But how do we achieve this fusion of art and promotion, passion and practicality? How do we create an authentic promotional campaign without surrendering to the demands of market trends or succumbing to the pressure of competition? In the following section, we will delve into these questions, bringing together theoretical insights, practical tips, and stoic philosophy to explore the craft of mindful marketing.

Value-Aligned Promotional Strategies

In order to grasp the depth of aligning promotional strategies with our personal values, we first need to ponder on the timeless questions that philosophers have dared to ask: What are our values? Why do they matter? How do they shape our actions? And, perhaps most crucially, how can they guide our brand attempting to market our work authentically?

Values, as much as they are personal, are the fundamental compass that orientates our decisions and actions. They seep into our work, whether deliberately or unintentionally. The key is to draw them into the surface of consciousness, understand them, and then harness their power with intentionality. By aligning your marketing strategies with your values, you give yourself the opportunity to create authentic promotions that represent you and connect with audiences on a deeper level. It is not a mere transaction of goods or services; you are communicating, sharing a part of yourself, your artwork — your passion. This alignment brings forth an authentic thread that weaves itself into every fabric of your creative venture.

For instance, if sustainability is a prominent value of yours, this could be encapsulated in eco-friendly packaging or promoting only in digital platforms to lessen carbon footprint. If community building matters to you, maybe your promotional events could involve activities that foster unity and camaraderie. Again, the values steering your ship will determine the route you take. There will be times when your values might clash with the norms or trending strategies in the market. It's in these challenging waves that the strength of your values tested. Hold your ground. Do not be swept away by the currents of societal expectations or competitors' tactics.

There is a profound power in authenticity. Authenticity resonates, it captivates its audience because it has a palpable sense of truth to it. People can see, feel, and appreciate authenticity. And when they do, they engage, not because they were lured by flashy, superfluous gimmicks, but because they found something genuine — something real to connect with. In the vast and often loud marketplace, where noise often drowns out substance, authenticity is refreshing, and it is compelling. By embedding your values into your promotional strategies, you create a voice that is uniquely yours, a voice that is heard, and a voice that is trusted. This trust, built upon the foundation of your values, extends beyond a solitary transaction; it forms the basis for continued interaction, for connection, and ultimately, for loyalty.

Marketing and Promoting Creative Work Effectively

At its core, marketing is about connection, a testament to human creativity woven into the tapestry of commerce and communication. You see, marketing isn't merely about shouting into the void, hoping for an echo. It's about crafting a narrative that resonates, about building a bridge between your inner world of creation and the outer world of consumer desires. This intersection is where authenticity meets strategy, birthing a promotion that feels less like a sales pitch and more like an invitation to a grand unveiling. The effective promotion of creative work relies on an intricate self-awareness and audience insight. You must know the rhythm of your own creative pulse just as well as you perceive the heartbeat of the market. This synergy allows for a promotional campaign that is attuned not only to what is being offered but also to why it matters.

Begin with your story—the authentic narrative that roots your work in personal soil. Humans are storytellers by nature; we seek connection through the shared tapestry of experiences. Let your audience peer behind the curtain. Show them the brushstrokes of your process, the scribbled lines of your drafts, the raw clay from which your sculptures arise. Let them feel the passion that fuels your late-night endeavors—the same passion that will ultimately call to them from the shelves and screens where your work awaits discovery. In this digital age, your online presence is a virtual gallery, a stage set for the world's eyes. Here, strategic use of social media platforms becomes paramount. Each post, tweet, or update serves as a collaborative brush stroke on the canvas of your brand. It is imperative to wield these tools with both intention and innovation, crafting content that sparks curiosity, provides content that connects without sacrificing the soul of your work. Balance this showcase with engagement, inviting dialogue and fostering relationships that extend beyond transactions and into the realm of community.

As you traverse the promotional landscape, remember that marketing, at its essence, is a form of education. You are teaching your audience not just about a product or service but about a perspective, a vision, an artistic truth. This requires a deep understanding of your audience's needs, desires, and challenges. Place yourself in their shoes, and when the time comes to speak, let your words meet their ears. The astute entrepreneur knows that promoting one's work is never a static endeavor. As the canvas of the market changes so too must your strategies adapt. Attend workshops, invest in courses, and absorb the insights of marketing mavens. Mix these lessons with your unique style to create an approach that is both agile and robust, ready to pivot with grace amid the shifting sands of industry demands. There exists a multitude of channels through which to amplify your voice: search engine optimization (SEO); email marketing; collaborations with fellow creatives amplify your chorus; and live events create a palpable buzz, transforming passive listeners into active participants.

Marketing is not merely a task to be checked off but an extension of the creative process itself. It calls for you to step into both the light and vulnerability, marrying the joy of creation with the strategic nous of exhibition. So venture forth, creative entrepreneur, with brush in hand and strategy at heart, into the marketplace that awaits your unique imprint on its ever-evolving canvas. And as you do, trust that your artistry—and the wisdom with which you share it—will leave indelible marks upon the hearts and minds of those you seek to inspire.

Chapter 18: Overcoming Financial Challenges and Building a Sustainable Creative Career

Financial Fundamentals

Many creative entrepreneurs, in the early stages of their journey, find themselves staring blankly at spreadsheets and puzzling over tax documents. Often, those who venture into the creative realm are met with a sudden, stark realization: finances matter, and they can be complex. Psychological wisdom has a role to play here, as does practicality. Therefore, we forge ahead into the terrains of fiscal landscapes.

The first aspect we explore in financial management is organization. Our financial life demands order much like our creative process. We must methodically arrange our income streams, our expenditures, and our savings. It's crucial to separate personal finances from business finances. An amalgamation of both realms often results in a confounding mess, leaving you overwhelmed and anxious.

Next comes budgeting. The mere mention of this term may evoke ponderous sighs coupled with a sense of dread. It is a crucial chapter in the story of our financial success. Budgeting involves making strategic decisions about where our money goes. Just as a sculptor chisels away excess marble to reveal a statue's true form, so too does an entrepreneur trim away unnecessary spending, molding financial wellness from the rough-cut stone of their business. It requires persistence, patience, and an insightful eye to see what the stone could become through reflective contemplation.

Bookkeeping, serves as the narrative basis of our financial story. It is the descriptive account of our financial journey – cataloguing where funds came from, where they traveled, and how they were utilized. Embrace it not as a burdensome task but as an insightful record of your entrepreneurial journey's aspect, a testament to your growth and evolution.

Finally, we consider taxes. This inevitable facet of financial life is shrouded in complexity. Yet, as with any journey through unknown lands, a map – in this case, a good accountant or tax software – can transform what was once daunting into manageable, navigable territory.

Remember to approach it as we do any significant creative endeavor. With patience, persistence, and an open mind, we can interpret the seemingly complicated financial management. By grasping these basic pillars of financial management, we establish both robust foundations and the assurance that sustains us as we continue to build our entrepreneurial empires. Our financial health becomes another measure of our success, and the authenticity of our journey.

Money Mangement and Planning

In a world that thrives on practicality and number crunching, money management and planning hold an unshakable significance. You may be an artist, a dreamer, a creator – all fuelled by passion and creativity, but beneath the canvas of your dreams flows a stream of financial realities that require your attention. Embracing these realities helps facilitating the creation of a sustainable artistic journey. Formulating a realistic and effective plan for managing your money is paramount. A financial plan acts as the compass guiding your entrepreneurial ship, steering it clear from the rocky shores of instability and toward the tranquil waters of sustainability.

Leaning on the wisdom from therapy, one must realize that anxiety around money management arises from a sense of uncertainty. To dispel this fog of uncertainty, the first step is to create a clear view of your financial picture. This requires a comprehensive assessment of your income streams, expenditure, savings, and debts.

Take pen to paper, or fingers to keyboard, and chart out your current assets and liabilities. Asses where your money comes from and where it goes. Are your current practices sustainable? Are there areas where adjustments are necessary? This reflective exercise will provide not just a snapshot of the current moment, but reveal patterns and trends that shape your approach to money. Remember, this is not a time to steep in judgement or be overwhelmed by the scale of your financial mountain. Instead, embrace a growth-oriented mindset. Celebrate the areas where you are thriving and commit to improving those that need attention. This exercise of honest evaluation is a cornerstone of financial health.

Central to money management is the setting of clear financial goals. These goals, much like in our creative pursuits, provide a sense of direction and a roadmap to success. Whether it is saving for a new art studio, investing in creative tools, or building an emergency fund, each goal serves as a guiding star aligning your financial decisions. While setting these goals, remember the strategic essence of entrepreneurialism. Balancing between short-term and long-term financial objectives, just as in creating art, one alternates between fine details and broader strokes. Goals must also reflect the dynamic nature of life and be flexible enough to accommodate unexpected alterations.

Financial management and planning might seem an alien concept to the creative mind, but, philosophical reflection reveals that this is merely another form of creativity. It requires strategic thinking, constant adaptation, and innovative problem-solving, all skills inherent in the entrepreneurial artist. Easing into the practice of money management and planning can lead to a sense of empowerment and control, resulting in reduced anxiety. Focusing the surge of anxiety to these practical chores can result in creative fuel for your entrepreneurship, making it a symbiotic relationship between art and resource. Taking a hold of your financial reality doesn't dilute your authenticity as a creative entrepreneur. On the contrary, it grounds your creativity in practicality, reinforcing the structure within which your creative freedom flourishes.

Focusing Anxiety to Practical Chores in Finance

So, where does our anxiety come from? The answer might not be extraordinary - it is the fear of the unknown, the unpredictable that jolts us more often than not. The erratic figures of our profits and losses, jumbled tax norms, or the daunting task of budgeting, they all contribute significantly to our anxiety. It's our unceremonious rendezvous with these unavoidable areas that necessitates arming ourselves with the shield of understanding and a sword of practical approach to slay the dragon of financial anxieties. When we talk about finance, know this: complexity is currency. But the good news is that complexity can be untangled, understood, and eventually, mastered. This understanding is the first step in transforming financial anxiety into financial efficacy. Financial literacy is a weapon, wielded to bring order to the chaos. This weapon isn't reserved for those with business degrees. As creatives, we too can, and indeed must, lay claim to it.

Think of it this way - managing finances shouldn't feel like a chore, but rather a necessity, an enabler. Suddenly you're not doing your taxes; you're mapping your financial journey. You're no longer just budgeting; you're setting the blueprint for your creative enterprise's growth. There's another side to this coin. The key isn't solely in the understanding of our finances; it's also in the application. So, how can we approach this arena practically, effectively?

Firstly, channel your creativity into your financial decisions. Make it a personal project, like creating a new piece of art or developing a business strategy. Design your budget like you would conceptualize an innovative marketing campaign. Learn the numbers, understand their rhythm, and creatively plot out your fiscal year.

Secondly, schedule regular financial check-ins. Just as we dedicate time and attention to our creative practices, so too should we dedicate it to our financial health. Regular awareness of our financial status provides stability and clarity, freeing up mental energy for our creative pursuits.

Finally, automate as much as possible. There are numerous financial management tools and apps available that can help ease the burden. Expenses can be tracked. Bills can be paid. Investments can be managed. By automating these tasks, we redirect our creative energy towards where it truly belongs — our artistic endeavors. The conversion of anxiety into practicality takes time, and it's a journey that varies for everyone. However, as we steadily tread this path, we'll find ourselves not just surviving, but thriving in the discordant symphony of entrepreneurship.

Tax and Legal Matters

Anxiety sets in when we fail to grasp that our creative ventures are not just an extension of our being, but also an entity subject to obligations before the law. As entrepreneurs, we must distil entrepreneurial insights to navigate through the labyrinth of tax regulations, sales permit requirements, licensing laws, and copyright considerations. When we begin to educate ourselves about tax entitlements and deductions that are relevant to us, we create a line of defense against financial anxiety and uncertainty. For instance, awareness that expenses incurred in the process of our venture, such as supplies, workspace costs, or even professional development courses, could potentially be tax-deductible helps our financial planning significantly.

While tax laws may appear complex and overwhelming, remember that they are designed to ensure fairness and ethics in our economic landscape. They are necessary companions on our entrepreneurial journey.

Parallel to tax are legal considerations - copyright laws are particularly pertinent for creative entrepreneurs. They provide us the shield to protect our ideas, our work, our creativity. They also delineate the boundaries within which we must operate to respect other creators' intellectual property. Understanding these laws can equip us with the confidence to share our work with the world and grow our businesses, fearlessly and authentically.

Embarking on self-education or seeking professional advice around these areas can help us to maneuver these complexities. Our mission is not to become legal experts or tax accountants, but to gain enough knowledge to direct our questions and concerns to those professionals who do specialize in these fields. By doing so, we turn our anxieties into focused actions, cultivating mental resilience. This expansive foundation of knowledge minimizes the risk of unexpected hurdles, freeing us to concentrate on our ultimate goal, which is nurturing our creative passions into a sustainable business.

Building a Financial Safety Net - Saving and Investing for the Future

It's no secret that money matters stimulate anxiety for many, and more so, for creative entrepreneurs who often walk on the razor's edge of financial instability. But let me assure you, it needn't be so. Building a financial safety net is imperative in this journey. The comfort offered by the knowledge that your future is secure, lucrative even, can alleviate much anxiety that often besets creative entrepreneurs. You might see this as a chore, an obligatory part of your creative journey, but I urge you to consider an alternative perspective, embrace it as a form of self-care. Saving and investing are not simply financially intelligent moves; they are acts of kindness you offer to your future self. When you save and invest, you're asserting faith in your own financial acuity, you're advocating for your future prosperity, you're reinforcing the authenticity of your entrepreneurial journey.

So where do you begin? Start with understanding your income flow. Know what comes in, know what goes out. Be mindful, reflective in your spending habits. A dollar saved today could well translate into more freedom to invest in your creativity tomorrow. Next, set aside a fraction of your income consistently. Let this be your safety net, your buffer against unexpected downturns. Gradually increase this fraction as your income expands. And then, venture into the realm of investing. Start with low-risk investments. A conservative approach to investing complements the inherent risks in creative entrepreneurship. Gradually move towards a more balanced portfolio, diversifying across industries and asset types. Remember, the tortoise does sometimes win the race. Slow and steady really can be a winning strategy in investment.

That said, do not let investing become an all-consuming beast that devours your creativity. Do not let it distract you from your passion, your artistry. Strive always for equilibrium. Balance your artistic aspirations with practical financial wisdom.

Diversifying Income and Revenue Sources

Diversification. A term so often evoked in financial circles, yet seldom explored in the realm of the artistic entrepreneur. Today, let us approach this concept with an open mind and an exploratory spirit. As creative entrepreneurs, we have the unique prospect of embracing diversification not merely as a financial strategy but as a tool for enhancing our creative expression. Diversifying your income streams doesn't necessarily mean juggling a multitude of projects at once or spreading oneself too thin. Instead, it's about strategically spreading your creative energies across multiple revenue channels. This strategy can offer financial stability, enhance your creative exposure, and provide a safety network in case one stream of income unexpectedly dries up.

Stability may seem as mythical as a unicorn grazing in a field of four-leaf clovers. But anchoring your financial well-being in the fertile soil of diversification is not only practical; it's an imperative strategy for today's creative entrepreneur. This increasingly vital aspect of your professional life begins by acknowledging a single, golden thread of truth: No single stream of income is a silver bullet capable of sustaining the ever-evolving nature of your work. To foster the economic resilience necessary for the storms of change and chance, one must weave a financial tapestry, rich with varied threads—each complementing, supporting, and enriching the others. The creation of multiple revenue sources invites you into a dance between creativity and pragmatism, a delicate balancing act that has been performed by history's most renowned artistic minds.

Take Leonardo da Vinci, a polymath whose insatiable curiosity birthed innovations across disciplines; his financial model was as intricate as the layers of "The Last Supper." His income was not solely tethered to the whims of his artistry; rather, he consulted, engineered, and envisioned across fields aplenty, ensuring sustenance for his creative endeavors. As modern day creators, how might we mirror Leonardo's mosaic of income streams? The process begins by looking inward, into the mirror of self-reflection, and asking ourselves: What skills, knowledge, or passions do we hold that can take on new life in the marketplace?

Consider writing an e-book or starting a blog where your expertise finds voice and value. Here, writing is not limited to mere catharsis, but becomes an offering—a sharing of wisdom that can weave income from readership or advertising. Expanding beyond the written word, one's artistry can also find new audiences through teaching. Online workshops or local classes become streams where knowledge flows from your creative reservoirs into the eager minds of others. This exchange is not merely transactional, but transformative, nurturing creativity within community walls and extending your influence beyond the canvas or keyboard. Perhaps you're a visual artist selling your paintings at local galleries. Diversifying might mean selling prints online alongside the originals. Or it might involve offering art workshops or tutorials, creating a passive income source through an online course, or even leveraging your art into merchandise like t-shirts or tote bags.

For writers, multiple revenue sources could mean self-publishing your work alongside traditional publishing, exploring freelance writing, creating audiobooks or podcast series, and many more. As with everything else in the creative entrepreneurial journey, the key is to be creative, innovative, and authentic in creating and developing these multiple streams of income. Licensing your work is another tributary to explore. Your art, whether visual or sonic, may resonate within commercial spaces, adorning products or complementing media, creating passive income as your creations journey through varied commercial terrains.

Merchandising opens doors to tangibility, bringing your brand into physical form through apparel, prints, or innovative products that echo your creative identity. Here, your creative signature becomes wearable, hangable, touchable.

Crowdfunding platforms and membership sites offer patrons the chance to directly support your work. This isn't merely a transaction; it's a pact between creator and community, where shared values and visions are exchanged for ongoing sustenance. Subscription models or exclusive content channels transform your consistent output into predictable income. In this garden, your most dedicated followers can harvest your newest creations, providing financial nutrients in return.

Collaborations and partnerships that cross-pollinate audiences and create symbiotic economic opportunities. These alliances magnify reach and revenue while spinning new stories within your creative universe.

Embracing this multitude of channels requires an entrepreneurial spirit to match your creativity—a spirit that reasons with resources, that embraces both the brushstroke and the spreadsheet with equal fervor. But remain vigilant; these streams must not erode the soul of your work but rather nourish it, must not dilute your essence but distill it. Therein lies the symphony of sustainability—a chorus of revenue streams not competing but completing one another, ensuring that your creative voice, bolstered by economic resilience, echoes into prosperity. In diversifying your income streams, remember that each new revenue source is like an instrument added to your symphonic repertoire. Together, they harmonize, supporting a financial melody that allows for the crescendos of success and buffers against the diminuendos of struggle.

Diversification is not just an economic strategy, it is a philosophical approach to embracing abundance in its various forms. Understanding that our creative potential is not limited to a single channel but vary through various outlets. Authentic diversification accepts, even celebrates, the idea of multiple ideas, multiple avenues, and multiple manifestations of a single creative impulse. As you reflect on this, take some time to brainstorm the different ways your creativity can be translated into diversified income streams. It's not merely about making more money—it's about creating a sustainable life that echoes your creative essence. For financial stability while being resilient in the face of uncertainty.

Thriving in a Creative Career

Embarking on the path of a creative entrepreneur is akin to nurturing a rare and delicate organism, one that thrives on passion yet demands the practical nourishment of financial wisdom. It is in the fusion of these two aspects—artistic fervor mingling with economic acumen—that a truly sustainable and thriving creative career blossoms. A sustainable career in creativity is more akin to a marathon than a sprint; it is a continuous evolution rather than a rapid ascension. In forging this career, it's crucial to adopt a multifaceted perspective, for the weight of financial burdens need not crush the spirit of the artist; it can be the very force that crafts a diamond out of coal.

Initially, sustainability may seem to conflict with the spontaneity of the artistic spirit. Yet, sustainable financial practices empower creativity by creating a secure platform from which leaps of artistic faith can be safely taken. The artist who conscientiously stewards their resources is free to explore the wilderness of imagination, knowing that their practical needs have been met. To cultivate this sustainable career, one must become strategic in the allocation of resources—time, energy, and money. Each of these is an investment, one that must be approached with the shrewdness of a merchant and the soul of a poet. Time is often the most elusive yet most valuable commodity. Mastery over one's schedule leads to increased productivity and offers space for the mind to wander through the fields of inspiration.

It is also through the keen application of marketing and promotion that a creative career gains traction. By harnessing the power of storytelling, one's work is elevated from mere commodity to an experience craved by an audience attentive to authenticity. The connection between creator and consumer becomes sacred—a relationship bound by mutual appreciation and underpinned by the currency of genuine engagement. The sustainable creative career is not merely a fortress against financial strife but a vessel for personal fulfillment and collective contribution. In this context, building partnerships with patrons and peers becomes a dance of mutual advancement. By sharing connections, resources, and expertise, creative entrepreneurs weave together a tapestry that shimmers with resilience and community spirit.

In these pages, we have not shied away from the storms that often assail creative careers. Yet we stand firm in the conviction that such careers can be both fruitful and enduring. The creative entrepreneur who masters the art of blending their craft with commerce is much like an alchemist, transforming the base metals of daily endeavor into enduring gold. As we reflect on what has been shared thus far, let us hold fast to this truth: A sustainable and thriving creative career is more than a dream—it is a tangible reality forged through the fires of passion tempered by the cool resolve of practical wisdom.

Practical Financial Planning for Creatives

The first practical step towards establishing a robust financial plan is understanding your current position. Pour over your income streams, expenditures, savings, and investments. What patterns do you notice? Are some expenditures unnecessary? Are there dormant income streams that can be activated?

The irregular income can be unpredictable, but with some strategic planning, it doesn't have to be unsettling. Maintaining a separate business account, setting aside a portion of your income for lean times, and creating a 'rainy day fund' can provide a cushion against financial anxiety. A savvy creative entrepreneur does not shy away from the idea of investment. This doesn't mean you have to plunge into the stock market—investments can be many and varied.

Perhaps a course to enhance your skills or upgrading your gear to boost productivity or even investing in a creative space that fuels your imagination.

In the realm of creative entrepreneurship, debt is a frequent visitor—be it for procuring materials, renting studio space, or investing in advertising. Dealing with debt requires a tactical approach. Prioritize repayments, starting with the highest interest rates. Restructure wherever possible and negotiate for lower interest rates. Remember, the aim is to minimize the anxiety accrued debt and instead, focus that energy on your creative pursuits.

And finally, let's broach the often-overlooked area of retirement planning. As creative entrepreneurs, we may imagine that we will 'create' indefinitely. But it's essential to respect our future selves and our future needs. Consider investment platforms, retirement funds, or even property investments. The choice is personal but reflection upon this matter is universal.

In this capitalist age, money is the language of exchange for goods and services. By addressing our attitudes towards it, strategic about its use and proactive in its management, we can transform financial planning from a source of angst to a tool of empowerment, fueling our creativity rather than hindering it.

Chapter 19: Cultivating a Positive Mindset and Wellbeing

Overcoming Perfectionism

We now turn to the art and discipline of cultivating a healthy mind and a nurtured spirit, hallmarked by a blend of self-compassion and a cessation from relentless perfectionism. The rubric for success as an entrepreneur or artist is often skewed towards perfection. Whether it's creating a masterpiece or delivering a stellar business pitch, the invisible threads of perfectionism tighten around us. However, in this incessant pursuit of precision, we often lose sight of the fundamental tenet of our humanity – our fallibility. This is where self-compassion swoops in as a gentle antidote to the caustic obsession with perfection, fundamentally transforming our creative journey.

Self-compassion, as an empowering construct, remains firmly rooted in the soil of three crucial components: self-kindness, mindfulness, and shared humanity. These elements, when incorporated can untangle the threads of perfectionism, setting us free in the decorated landscape of creative solace.

Self-kindness extends beyond merely being lenient to oneself; it is a warm embrace of acceptance, acknowledging our shortcomings and celebrating our strengths simultaneously. As a creative entrepreneur, embracing self-kindness means recognizing that your artistic prowess and entrepreneurial spirit are neither magnified by your triumphs nor diminished by your setbacks.

Borrowing from the wisdom of psychology, mindfulness can be envisioned as a pragmatic invitation to reside in the present moment, devoid of judgment or criticism. In the context of overcoming perfectionism, practicing mindfulness grants us the freedom to detach our worth from external validation. It reminds us that our value does not flow with the tide of societal expectations or external successes. Mindfulness enables us to see ourselves as we truly are - a living hybrid of potentials, vulnerabilities, and triumphs. Reflecting on shared humanity, and the interconnectedness of our emotional experiences, reminds us that we are not alone in our journey. Failure, frustration, and self-doubt are not solitary voyagers who have chosen your ship alone; they pay a visit to every artist and entrepreneur, making our journey collectively human. Recognizing this shared humanity liberates us, as we lean into the comforting knowledge that even in our most vulnerable moments, we are united in our struggles and our resilience.

Overcoming perfectionism is not about lowering your standards or abandoning the pursuit of excellence. Instead, it is about redefining success - not as a flawless victory but as the courage to dance with vulnerability, to engage with failure, and to rise - stronger and wiser.

You are not a machine calibrated for incessant perfection but a resilient artist on a journey of continuous evolution amidst the harmonious symphony of triumphs and failures.

Cultivating gratitude and Joy in the Creative Process

In the maelstrom of work, deadlines, pressures, and expectations, the simple joy of the creative process itself can get obscured. Buried beneath layers of anxiety, self-doubt, and worry. But those who learn to rekindle that joy, to keep it burning even in the darkest of times – they are the ones who truly thrive. So, how do we reclaim this joy? How do we cultivate gratitude amidst the trials and tribulations of our creative journey?

The answer lies within us. It's housed within the resilient chambers of our heart, within the creative soul that chose to reach beyond the ordinary, risking vulnerability for creation. This is where the practice of gratitude comes in, as a counterbalance to the rigors of creative entrepreneurship. Gratitude is about recognizing and cherishing the abundance in our lives. It is about shifting our focus from what's missing or imperfect to what's already present and beautiful. It is about celebrating not just the milestones but also the small, seemingly insignificant triumphs – the completion of a project, a compliment from a client, or the sheer simplicity of a good idea coming to life.

But gratitude isn't just a buzzword we casually toss around; it's a deliberate practice, a conscious choice that influences our perspective. It involves noting down these moments of thankfulness regularly, even on difficult days (especially on difficult days!). A gratitude journal is an effective tool to facilitate this process. The act of writing down can be therapeutic in itself, helping anchor these positive feelings into our conscious and subconscious mind. As we practice gratitude, we'll notice a shift. A shift in mindset, a shift in mood. A sense of fullness will replace emptiness, contentment will elbow out dissatisfaction. This might not eliminate the challenges, but it will certainly arm us better to face them.

Now, let's turn to the second part of our journey – finding joy in the creative process. While it may sound straightforward, it's often easier said than done. In a society that measures success in terms of tangible outputs and accolades, delighting in the process can seem like an indulgence. But remember, the journey is as important, if not more, than the destination. Finding joy in the creative process is about cherishing the act of creation for its own sake. It's about embracing curiosity and wonder, about letting the mind wander, make connections, and revel in the sheer pleasure of creating. It's about drenching ourselves in the experience, be it writing a thought-provoking article, designing an aesthetic layout, or coding a complex software.

Each stroke of the brush, each keystroke, each note played on an instrument - they are not just steps towards the final work; they are intimate dances with our creative spirit, an affirmation of our unique capabilities to perceive, conceive and express. Finding joy in the creative process is about immersing ourselves fully in the act of creating, without being overly fixated on the end product. It's about treasuring the learning and growth that takes place along the journey.

While the creative journey is characterized by highs and lows, it is the gratitude for every tiny step forward and the joy in the very act of creating that make the rollercoaster worthwhile.

Focus on Physical Health and Wellness

It's a story often repeated, a stereotype so entrenched that it has become a cultural trope—the artist sacrificing themselves, ignoring physical needs and wellbeing in the quest for the elusive masterpiece. This image of the suffering artist is not only dramatic but dangerously misleading. To thrive we must recognize the inextricable link between body and mind, to appreciate that our physical health has a profound impact on our mental health.

Think of your body as your vessel in this journey. A poorly maintained vessel, neglecting its needs for repair, rest, and maintenance, will break down before reaching the destination. The same is true for our physical bodies—they carry us through life, supporting our mind and spirit in this journey. Our bodies are not mere vessels though, they are our partners, eloquent speakers if we make a habit to listen. They communicate to us the signs of stress, fatigue, and imbalance, often long before our minds register these messages. Our bodies, guide us toward resilience, and wellbeing.

Prioritizing physical health and wellbeing starts with the basics—adequate sleep, a balanced diet, and regular physical activity. Sleep refreshes our minds, diet fuels our bodies, and physical activity rejuvenates both. Yet, in the rush and thrill of building a dream, these fundamental needs can be overlooked. Sleep is not a luxury—it's an absolute necessity. It's sleep that renews our brain cells, repairs our bodies and restores our energy. Adequately rested, we awaken to our full potential. We are more constructive, more productive, more creative.

Our diet too plays a pivotal role in maintaining our physical health. A balanced diet, rich in fruits, vegetables, and whole grains, provides the nutrients essential for optimal brain function and energy. The therapeutic wisdom says, "We are what we eat". This wisdom holds true for our mental health as well. What we consume directly affects our mood, cognition, and behavior. Imagine the impact of high-performance fuel on a high-performance vehicle – that's the power of a balanced diet on your body.

Regular physical activity, the third pillar of physical health, is not merely about maintaining physical fitness. It is a therapeutic tool, a philosophical practice, a canvas where we paint our resilience. Whether it's a brisk walk in the park, yoga in the quiet of the morning, or a high-intensity workout session, physical activity rejuvenates our mind, sharpens our cognition, and fortifies our emotional resilience.

Invest in your body. Treat it with respect, nurture it with good food, rest, and activity. Listen to it when it speaks to you. Prioritizing physical health is not a sideline activity—it's a core strategy for your entrepreneurial journey—a strategy that prepares you not just to survive, but to thrive. It's time to dismantle the myth of creativity thriving on suffering. Let's replace it with a new narrative—a narrative where our physical health and wellbeing serve as the foundation of our creative endeavors and entrepreneurial success.

Seeking Professional Support

Life as a creative entrepreneur is akin to reading a novel laden with twists and turns. In one chapter, we may find ourselves basking in the intoxicating euphoria of success, and in the next, we grapple with the unnerving uncertainties of failure. Yet, as our narrative unfolds, there evolves an inherent paradox of the human spirit: our resilience in the face of adversity, our capacity to convert it into an engine of creativity, and our often unrecognized need to share it with those who can guide us through, professionally. Recognizing the need for professional help, and more importantly, seeking it out, is an act of strength. It is an assertion of self-worth and a testament to our innate desire for continued growth and self-actualization. Anxiety, burnout, and the various psychological components of our creative journey are not simply obstacles to overcome. They are complex issues that need attention, understanding, and often, expert intervention.

Therapists equip us with tools to wordlessly communicate with our subconscious, explore the hidden alcoves of our minds, and set free our potential even amidst seemingly unwinnable battles. Psychotherapy is not merely a refuge for the troubled mind. It is an academy for every creative soul seeking to unravel the intricate tapestry of their thoughts, emotions, feelings, and behaviors. The entrepreneurial environment can at times resemble a gladiator's arena, where each day presents an array of battles to face. In such situations, coaching evolves as our trusted mentor—a personal guide that helps us navigate our creative journey with clarity and resilience. Coaches work to build upon our intrinsic strengths, bring structure to our wildest dreams, and steer us not only towards financial success but also towards emotional, intellectual, and spiritual enrichment.

Validation and support also emerge from unanticipated corners, such as support groups. These are a compendium of empathetic souls who, like us, balance on the tightrope of ambition and self-doubt. Engaging with them allows us to rise above the clouded illusion of isolation and witness our shared, human experience. Each story, each journey breathes life into the reassuring truth that we are not alone in our quest for personal and professional fulfillment. The path to authenticity is not devoid of stress and strife, but neither must it be traversed alone. There is wisdom in collaborating with specialists whose insights enhance our self-understanding and fortify our mental resilience. The choice to seek help is not an admission of failure; instead, it is an affirmation of our determination to thrive amid challenges.

In the grand theatre of life, we are the playwrights of our stories, with the liberty to call upon the guidance of a discerning director. So, let us not shirk from seeking professional help and support when needed. For it is in learning to say 'I need help' that we come to understand the profound strength that lies in vulnerability.

Chapter 20: Sustaining Thriving: Long-Term Strategies for Creative Entrepreneurs

Building Longevity Self-Care Habits

Here we will delve into the art of nurturing resilience and self-care routines: these are your safeguards against the tempests of the industry, your personal anthem of enduring grace.

The Japanese have a term, "Kintsugi," that beautifully captures the essence of resilience. When a piece of pottery breaks, instead of discarding it, artisans mend the cracks with gold, creating a tapestry of shining veins. This transformation not only repairs the pottery but also celebrates its history, strength, and unique beauty. We too must learn the art of Kintsugi within our own lives; we must infuse the cracks in our journey with gold, finding strength in our repairs, and beauty in our resilience. Resilience is not a static attribute but a pulsating rhythm that injects vitality into the creative spirit. It is the quiet determination that inspires us to rise with the morning dew and approach our canvas anew, regardless of yesterday's discarded drafts. Just as resilience needs to be nurtured, self-care cannot be relegated to the periphery of our sundry tasks; it is the axis upon which our creative worlds spin.

Begin by honoring the sacred within the mundane. A morning walk, the gentle infusion of green tea into hot water, or simply a moment of silence amid the cacophony of the waking world—these acts are not trifles to be dismissed. They are the silent guardians of our mental sanctuary, small yet mighty sentinels that protect our wellbeing. In these routines lies a powerful antidote to the brew of chaos that oft besets our entrepreneurial path. Next, we must embed these routines within the sinewy fabric of our daily lives, ensuring they sustain not just for weeks or months, but for a lifetime. This might mean setting inviolable hours for rest and reflection or pledging a day each week to the rejuvenation of mind, body, and spirit. Herein lies not just prevention against burnout, but a proactive stride towards flourishing vitality.

At the heart of resilience is the concept of 'bouncing back'—a phrase that belies the elegance of its implications. To bounce back from adversity does not suggest a mere return to form. It signifies a transcendence: the ability to emerge from challenges not only unscathed but enriched, sculpted into a more intricate and robust version of oneself.

Let us then embark on cultivating this elasticity of spirit by recognizing that self-care is not indulgence—it is the very bedrock of sustainability. Your self-care routine need not be elaborate or time-consuming; it can be as simple as moments of stillness before the onslaught of dawn, the ritualistic savoring of a midday coffee, or the nightly surrender to literature that nourishes your soul. This gentle tending to self is a strategy as ancient as the philosophies that have long contemplated the human condition. Like Sisyphus knowingly embracing his eternal task, we must acknowledge that there will be days when our resilience feels as heavy as the boulder itself. It is here, in this acknowledgment, that we find the strength to push ever onward, to thrive not despite the weight but because of our unwavering commitment to ourselves.

To solidify these practices, we venture into the realm of ritual. The ritual, both sacred and secular, is a testament to the human desire for order and meaning. Your self-care ritual need not be steeped in incense or shrouded in mystique—it merely requires a consistent differentiation from the mundane. By anchoring your self-care in routine, you are guaranteeing yourself a touchstone in times of turbulence, a personal haven that can be accessed irrespective of outer chaos. This sanctuary is not a place of escape but rather a fortification—it enables you to marshal your resources, both internal and external, and fortifies you for re-entry into the fray with renewed vigor.

Creating a Long-Term Motivation Plan

To maintain the light of creativity, you must craft a personalized long-term plan, a blueprint for the motivation that propels you forward. First, let's recognize that motivation is not a constant companion. Like the phases of the moon, it waxes and wanes. Yet, its cyclical nature need not become a harbinger of inertia; rather, it is an invitation to understand the rhythms of your creative spirit and to plan accordingly. Your long-term motivation hinges on crafting a narrative for your future self—a narrative that resonates with the core of who you are and who you aspire to become.

Begin with reflection. Consider the milestones you've already reached and the hurdles you've overcome. What drove you forward in those moments? Was it passion for your craft? The thrill of overcoming challenges? Or perhaps the satisfaction derived from impacting others through your work? Every past motivation holds a clue to your future drive. From this introspective endeavor, distill the essence of what propels you. Next, envision your future. Where do you see your work taking you? What impact do you want to have on your industry, your community, the world at large? Envisioning is not idle daydreaming but rather a strategic visualization. By projecting your aspirations onto the canvas of tomorrow, you begin to see the possible paths that lie ahead. This vision becomes the beacon that guides your motivation through the fog of uncertainty.

Now, transform vision into objectives. Divide your overarching goals into attainable targets. Set benchmarks for progress, not as rigid constraints but as stepping stones across the river of your creative journey. As you map out these goals, infuse each with personal significance—why each milestone matters deeply to you. This emotional resonance is the fuel for sustained motivation. This long-term motivation plan should be a living document— one that breathes with the cadence of your creative pulse. Revisit it frequently, revising it to capture newly discovered passions or lessons learned. Reflect on your progress and celebrate each achievement, no matter how small, for each success is a reaffirmation of your capabilities and a wellspring of continued motivation.

Above all, embed within your plan those rituals that sustain you—the quiet moments of reflection, the bursts of spontaneous creativity, and the celebrations with those who journey alongside you. These are not mere indulgences; they are vital to nurturing the joy and fulfillment that feed your motivation.

Cultivating a Creative Community

As we traverse the winding path, often one of the most overlooked yet integral components to sustainability is fostering a supportive and collaborative creative community. Creative work, by its very nature, is a solitary pursuit. It's a dance between the self and the canvass of creation, a dance of ideas and execution. This can sometimes lure the creative entrepreneur into an illusion of isolation, an erroneous belief in the fallacy of the wandering, lone genius. Worse yet, the competitive nature of entrepreneurship can further alienate us from our peers, engendering an atmosphere of rivalry rather than solidarity. However, an emphasis on community ushers in a symbiotic ecosystem of mutual growth and support. Fostered wisely, it can become the social bedrock upon which your creative ventures stand resilient amidst unpredictable entrepreneurial terrain.

Firstly, understand that your creative journey need not be ensnared by competition. While it is true that entrepreneurship is often framed within the Darwinian jungle of survival of the fittest, the reality is more nuanced and far less fatalistic. In the realm of the creative, the concepts of competition and value proposition are intimately linked - not to the extent of your superiority over others, but rather in your unique ability to offer something distinct and captivating. Every creative entrepreneur brings to the table a profound individuality, a unique blend of experiences, perspectives, and insights that no other can replicate. Recognize this, and you elevate your peers from competitors to potential collaborators on this artistic voyage.

Secondly, genuinely invest in your community. Authentic relationship-building requires more than superficial networking; it demands a sincere interest in others' works, challenges, and triumphs. Remember that empathy is the cornerstone of lasting relationships. Appreciate the struggles and successes of your colleagues as you would your own. Listen, not with the intent to reply, but purely to understand, and respond accordingly. As paradoxical as it may sound, you should aim to become a selfless entrepreneur in an inherently self-driven pursuit.

Thirdly, adopt a philosophy of giving. Bear in mind the wisdom from the age-old adage that 'giving is receiving.' Nurture your creative community not just for the potential synergies and collaborations it offers, but also because there is immense satisfaction in its fostering. Share your knowledge freely, offer assistance generously, inspire others relentlessly. Your community will repay your kindness tenfold in ways you cannot envision - through inspiration, through opportunities, and through shared strength in times of tribulation.

Self-Reflection and Growth

Consider this: every piece of art that you create, every business decision that you make, is like a mirror that reflects a part of who you are. As artists and entrepreneurs, when we create something new, we reveal a bit of ourselves through it. Therefore, our creations - works of art or business ventures - can serve as potent tools for self-discovery and self-improvement if we dare to look closely. The process of creating - be it a painting or a product - is often accompanied by a whirlwind of emotions and thoughts. This emotional and cognitive overload can sometimes cloud our ability to see clearly. However, if we consciously strive to create a habit of reflective introspection, we can examine these feelings and thoughts to uncover insights about ourselves and our creative processes.

It is essential to pause and reflect - asking ourselves critical questions such as: What worked well for this project? In which areas did I feel challenged? How did I respond to these challenges? What emotional or mental roadblocks did I encounter? What fueled my inspiration throughout this process? The answers to these questions serve as a guidepost, leading us toward areas where growth and development are possible. They help us identify our strengths and areas of improvement, provide clarity on our emotional responses, and reveal insights into our creative triggers. Keep in mind; it is not enough to merely ask these questions. We must also be willing to listen, to accept, and to act on the answers no matter how daunting they may be. The ability to face our shortcomings with honesty and grace is the first step towards growth and self-improvement.

Engage in this kind of reflective thinking, not just at the end of a significant project, but also on a regular day-to-day basis. Take time each day, perhaps during the twilight hours of early morning or late evening, to sit quietly with your thoughts and reflect. Ask yourself: What inspired me? What did I learn? How did I grow? Such a practice encourages a state of mindfulness, promoting a sense of presence, acceptance, and adaptability. We are molded by our experiences. Every stroke of the paintbrush, every business decision made, is an imprint of our journey - a testament to our evolving self. By practicing continuous self-evaluation and reflection, we do not merely observe this evolution; we actively participate in it.

Final Chapter: Thriving Beyond Limits: a Call to Action

The Potential for Creative Entrepreneurs to Thrive.

Creative entrepreneurship is an odyssey— not a sprint nor a solo marathon, but a community relay. The journey is undeniably filled with explosive sparks of inspiration, searing bouts of anxiety, scorching moments of self-doubt, and the kindling warmth of accomplishment. I've endeavored throughout this book to illuminate the path, providing insight into the power of authenticity and mental resilience in painting a vivid picture of creative entrepreneurship.

Plato, the grand doyen of philosophy, once poignantly stated that "the measure of a man is what he does with power." The creative mind, for all its vulnerabilities, possesses an immense power. It can conceive something where nothing was before, it can manifest ideas into reality — a rare magic held by the artist, the entrepreneur, the creator. Yet at times, that power is obscured by the fog of anxiety, a specter looming large over many a creative mind. By now, it should be clear that this common foe of anxiety isn't an insurmountable force. Rather, it can become a catalyst, propelling you towards authenticity, towards growth. A phoenix rising from the ashes of self-doubt and criticism and transforming them into the brilliant flame of self-awareness and belief.

Recall the stories discussed throughout this book: the artist grappling with self-doubt and imposter syndrome; the entrepreneur teetering on the tightrope between passion and practicality; and their eventual victory against these challenges. Each narrative serves as a testament to one unifying truth: creative entrepreneurs are indeed predisposed to anxiety, but they are also incredible resilient, capable of thriving in the face of adversity. The entrepreneurial environment is dynamic, often volatile. This uncomfortable reality is probably no stranger to you. Yet, within its unpredictable contours lies the potential for astounding creativity. The tides of challenge and success, they all play a role in shaping the entrepreneur, the artist, the creator you are and will become.

The metaphorical arena where you wrestle with anxiety, face your critics, and emerge unscathed — this is where you become real. This is where authenticity thrives. As you have read in the previous chapters, separating your creative pursuit from the associated anxiety can seem daunting, but remember the practical wisdom lingered in those pages. As we close this chapter of our conversation, I encourage you to hold steadfastly to these lessons learned. They form the foundation to a central message: yes, creative entrepreneurship is challenging; it's rife with obstacles, but it's also ripe with opportunities.

A Call to Action to for Mixing Therapy, Philosophy, and Practical wisdom

We are driven by an innate curiosity, a continuously burning desire to express and shape the world in our own unique way. Shall we not then, seize the opportunity to craft our own journey, underscored by mental resilience and authenticity? The call to action, beckons you to embrace a fusion of therapy, philosophy, and practical wisdom in your journey ahead. Therapy, both professionally guided and self-initiated, serves as a flashlight in the obscurity of our minds. It gently illuminates the unfrequented corners of our psyche, inviting exploration and comprehension. It stimulates self-realization, the fulcrum upon which the scales of mental health and wellbeing pivot. Therapy encourages us to examine our anxiety triggers, our self-doubt, and our personal narratives with a compassionate lens, ultimately equipping us with the cognitive and emotional tools needed to navigate the entrepreneurial terrain.

On the other hand, philosophy offers solace and, indeed, companionship. It proffers the comforting thought that we are not alone in our struggles, in our questions of existence and meaning—those who came before grappled with them too, and those who come after will continue to do so. It urges us to redefine success, to scrutinize the confines of societal expectations and dare to carve our path. Philosophy is both the result of critical thinking and its catalyst, a beacon of wisdom lighting our way forward. However essential therapy and philosophy might be, we must remember that they are most effective when coupled with practical wisdom. The marriage of insight with action forges the path towards transformation. It assists us in translating our thoughts and introspections into tangible behaviours and habits. By applying the lessons learned from therapy and philosophy, practical wisdom ensures our personal growth doesn't remain in the abstract realm but manifests itself in our everyday reality.

Share this Newfound Knowledge with the Creative Community

The wisdom you've accrued - this blend of therapeutic insights, philosophical reflections, and practical strategies - forms a beacon of light in the often tumultuous sea that is the creative industry. It's a lighthouse that can guide others who are adrift, searching for their own landmarks amidst the foggy waters of entrepreneurship. You now have the power to revolutionize your creative community. You have the power to bestow hope, to share strength, to permeate resilience. As you pass milestones on your unique journey to authenticity, your story becomes part of the tapestry that makes up our shared experience. We are all interconnected, each strand of our individual narratives weaving together, creating a beautiful, rich, and complex picture.

There is an unspoken understanding between creative individuals. A silent recognition of the marvels and the hardships that come along with the desire to create. When you share your insights, your triumphs, your stumbling blocks and ways you've found to navigate them, you touch upon the invisible thread that binds us all. You encourage creative dialogue within our community, which then blossoms into solidarity, enriching our collective resilience. As we move forward beyond the boundaries of this book, it is my hope that you'll embrace the power of that shared experience. In sharing your unique journey from anxiety to authenticity, you can offer valuable mental health resources to others in the creative world. You can help to destigmatize mental health discussions and normalize therapeutic practices and philosophy within our everyday lives. By being open about your battles, by acknowledging their existence openly, you permit others to do the same.

Standing before you is a platform. A platform to communicate your journey, a platform to share the knowledge you have gleaned from resilience in the face of adversity, a platform to inspire. As you step up to address your community, arm yourself with your hard-earned wisdom. Speak with confidence, speak with authenticity, but most of all, speak with the understanding that your words can become someone else's guiding light.

By sharing this book and it's messages, you create a ripple effect that encourages others to share too, and together, we build a community where mental health is not taboo but part of the everyday dialogue. Where the journey from anxiety to authenticity is recognized as an integral part of the creative process, not an anomaly to be hidden away. And so, take up the torch, and shine its light outwards, for sharing is the conduit through which isolation is dissolved, and comradeship is born. Through this sharing, we can change the narrative of struggling alone and instead build supportive structures that allow us all to flourish creatively.

Printed in Great Britain
by Amazon

c5b975a4-5646-4710-8f85-c38414ec2d3aR01